DUTCH AND FLEMISH PAINTINGS
FROM THE HERMITAGE

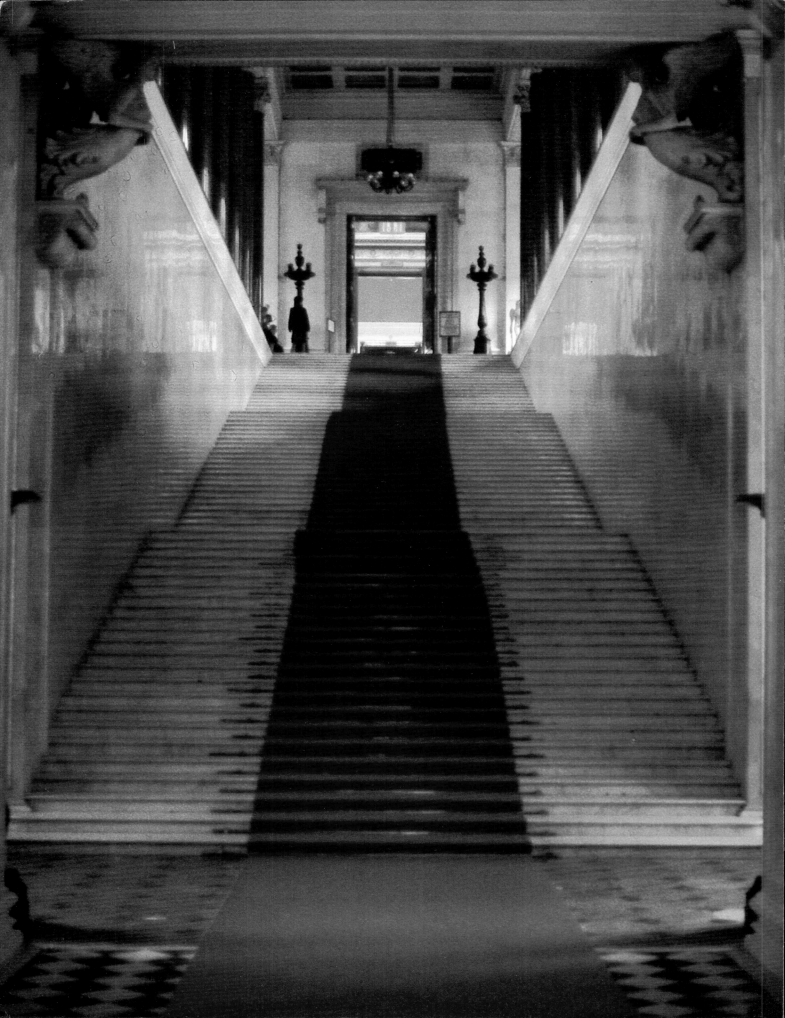

DUTCH AND FLEMISH PAINTINGS FROM THE HERMITAGE

THE METROPOLITAN MUSEUM OF ART
New York

THE ART INSTITUTE OF CHICAGO

Distributed by Harry N. Abrams, Inc., New York

This publication was issued in connection with the exhibition *Dutch and Flemish Paintings from the Hermitage*, held at The Metropolitan Museum of Art from March 26, 1988, to June 5, 1988, and at The Art Institute of Chicago from July 9, 1988, to September 18, 1988. This exhibition was made possible by Sara Lee Corporation.

Published by The Metropolitan Museum of Art, New York
John P. O'Neill, Editor in Chief
Kathleen Howard, Editor
Gerald Pryor, Designer
Gwen Roginsky, Production Manager

Type set by U.S. Lithograph, typographers, New York
Printed and bound by Arti Grafiche Amilcare Pizzi, S.p.a., Milan, Italy

Frontispiece: The Hermitage—main staircase. Photo: James N. Wood
Front cover: Detail of no. 26; Rembrandt van Rijn, *Haman Recognizes His Fate (David and Uriah?)*
Back cover: The Hermitage, Leningrad

Library of Congress Cataloging-in-Publication Data

Dutch and Flemish paintings from the Hermitage, Leningrad.
      p.   cm.
    Catalog of an exhibition to be held in March 1988.
    Bibliography: p.
ISBN 0-87099-509-X; ISBN 0-87099-510-3 (pbk.);
ISBN 0-8109-1139-6 (Abrams: hard)
    1. Painting, Dutch—Exhibitions. 2. Painting, Modern—17th–18th centuries—Netherlands—Exhibitions. 3. Painting, Flemish—Exhibitions. 4. Painting, Modern—17th–18th centuries—Flanders—Exhibitions. 5. Gosudarstvennyĭ Ėrmitazh (Soviet Union)—Exhibitions. I. Gosudarstvennyĭ Ėrmitazh (Soviet Union) II. Art Institute of Chicago. III. Metropolitan Museum of Art (New York, N.Y.)

ND636.D9 1988
759.9492′074′074—dc19   87-31252
                                       CIP

CONTENTS

FOREWORD

The Hermitage is pleased to present to the American public an exhibition of master-pieces by Dutch and Flemish painters of the seventeenth century. The paintings in the exhibition are all of the highest quality and have been selected to reflect the diversity of the Hermitage collections.

The exhibition includes six works by the great painter Rembrandt van Rijn, among them *The Holy Family* (no. 25) and the *Portrait of an Old Jew* (no. 27). Of equal interest are five paintings by Peter Paul Rubens in various genres, including *The Adoration of the Shepherds* (no. 44) and *Landscape with Stone Carriers* (no. 46), and two important oil sketches, *The Arch of Ferdinand* (no. 47) and *The Arch of Hercules* (no. 48). Visitors to the exhibition will certainly admire Gerard ter Borch's *Catrina van Luenink* (no. 3) and *A Glass of Lemonade* (no. 4). Another painting worth particular attention is Frans Hals's *A Young Man Holding a Glove* (no. 11), part of the Gotzkovsky collection, which was purchased in 1764 and whose acquisition marked the foundation of the Hermitage collections, soon to celebrate their 225th anniversary.

The establishment of contacts with American museums and the exchange of exhibitions have been most satisfying developments for us. In 1986, for example, the United States sent to the Hermitage the impressive exhibition *Masterpieces of French Painting from the First Half of the Nineteenth Century to the Early Twentieth Century*, and a large exhibition devoted to the Impressionists and twentieth-century French painters traveled to the United States.

The Hermitage is confident that the proposed exchanges of art exhibitions will strengthen the trust and friendship between the peoples of the Soviet Union and the United States.

I would like to offer my thanks to the administrative staffs of the two American museums that helped to organize the exhibition.

Boris Piotrovsky
Director
The Hermitage

FOREWORD

In August 1975 an agreement was signed between The Metropolitan Museum of Art and the U.S.S.R. Ministry of Culture establishing a series of exchange exhibitions. The excitement that greeted this event in the United States, especially in New York City, was intense, since the American people knew that in short order they would have an opportunity to see the unparalleled riches of such legendary museums as the Pushkin, the Hermitage, and the Kremlin. They were not disappointed. A matchless exhibition of Scythian gold in 1975 was followed by a lavish display of Russian costumes. Two years later we were introduced to Russian and Soviet paintings, and in 1979 enameled and jeweled wonders from the Kremlin were presented.

In return the Soviet people enjoyed an exhibition of one hundred of the finest paintings in the Metropolitan Museum, which was followed by examples from the Metropolitan's holdings of pre-Columbian gold, a selection of American Realist paintings from its American Wing, and a number of works from its Classical collections.

With the signing of a new cultural agreement by General Secretary Gorbachev and President Reagan at the Geneva summit meeting in 1985, the way was prepared for a renewal of exchanges. In due course a fresh protocol was issued by the U.S.S.R. Ministry of Culture and two American museums, the Metropolitan and The Art Institute of Chicago. The protocol specified two exchanges from each country to be realized during the next several years. This exhibition of Dutch and Flemish paintings from the Hermitage is the first of the Soviet exchanges. As it makes its tour of New York and Chicago, a reciprocal exhibition of French nineteenth-century and early twentieth-century paintings will open to audiences in Moscow and Leningrad; of the fifty-one canvases from the United States, thirty have been selected from The Art Institute of Chicago, with the balance from The Metropolitan Museum of Art.

In addition, in 1989–90 we have made a commitment to share with the U.S.S.R. examples of art from the Medieval collections of the Metropolitan Museum and the Art Institute, and the U.S.S.R. Ministry of Culture has graciously agreed to lend us some of their finest works of French painting from the early seventeenth to the twentieth century in an exhibition titled *Poussin to Matisse*.

Both of these exchanges have been made possible with the generous support of Sara Lee Corporation. We are grateful to John H. Bryan, Jr., Chairman and Chief

Executive Officer of Sara Lee Corporation, for his personal interest in these exhibitions and for the early commitment that has allowed us to proceed with their realization.

The Dutch and Flemish pictures in the Hermitage comprise one of the greatest collections of Northern European paintings anywhere and illustrate an important chapter in the history of collecting and connoisseurship since about 1700. Peter the Great, as noted in the introduction, included the Netherlands in his Western travels of 1696 and 1718, when he purchased paintings by Rubens, Rembrandt, Jan Steen, Adriaen van Ostade, and such favorites of eighteenth-century amateurs as Philips Wouwerman and Pieter van der Werff. The czar's agents maintained an ambitious program of acquisitions in Holland and at Antwerp and Brussels, but their efforts now appear as a mere prelude to the extraordinary purchases of pictures, and entire collections, by Catherine the Great after her accession to the throne in 1762. Her passionate pursuit of works of art, which involved the most distinguished connoisseurs and critics of the eighteenth century, tends to obscure the achievements of later periods, when the Hermitage gradually evolved into a museum and continued to expand rapidly in an increasingly scholarly fashion. For example, the methodically amassed collection of Petr Semenov-Tianshansky, which included some seven hundred Dutch and Flemish paintings, was acquired in 1910, adding almost two hundred names to the list of Northern artists represented in the Hermitage. Today the Hermitage's collection is a vast and comprehensive repository that contains some of the supreme masterpieces of Western art.

We are of course delighted that after a hiatus of ten years we once again have the opportunity to display some of the greatest works of art from the most celebrated Soviet museums, and it is our fond hope that the overtures and agreements following in the wake of the cultural agreement of 1985 will prove to be only a harbinger of things to come.

Philippe de Montebello
Director
The Metropolitan Museum of Art

James N. Wood
Director
The Art Institute of Chicago

SPONSOR'S FOREWORD

In 1981 I had the good fortune to visit Leningrad for the first time. There, in the city that has been called "the Venice of the North," I was struck by the pervasiveness of the magical light. Citizens gathered at dusk in the famed Summer Garden to read poetry, while colors deepened on the walls of eighteenth-century palaces designed by Italian architects. Observing these sights, I was reminded of the historical importance of Leningrad: Peter the Great conceived his capital to be a seat of power and an international gateway. Diderot, Berlioz, and Mahler are among some of the world's great thinkers who at one time lived in Leningrad, inspired by its illumination and by the drama of its history.

It is only fitting, then, that some of the finest seventeenth-century Dutch and Flemish canvases are housed in Leningrad's Hermitage, for the old masters were above all concerned with exploring illumination as a spiritual phenomenon. The glow suffusing a church nave, the gleam in the eye of a cavalier, the shimmering surface of a canal—all were part of the special province of Rembrandt, van Ruisdael, van Dyck, and their compatriots. Their paintings are touchstones of universal communication, allowing us, as Marcel Proust observed, "to see the world multiply until we have before us as many worlds as there are original artists."

Since that first trip to Leningrad, I have hoped that the old master paintings of the Hermitage would someday come to the United States. Sara Lee Corporation is proud to help bring these masterpieces to this country in an unprecedented exchange of exhibitions between the Hermitage and two outstanding American institutions —The Metropolitan Museum of Art and The Art Institute of Chicago. We at Sara Lee aspire to the originality, quality, and talent evident in the plans of beautiful cities and the works of master painters, and we are honored to contribute to a continuing international dialogue conducted in the spirit of great art.

John H. Bryan, Jr.
Chairman and Chief Executive Officer
Sara Lee Corporation

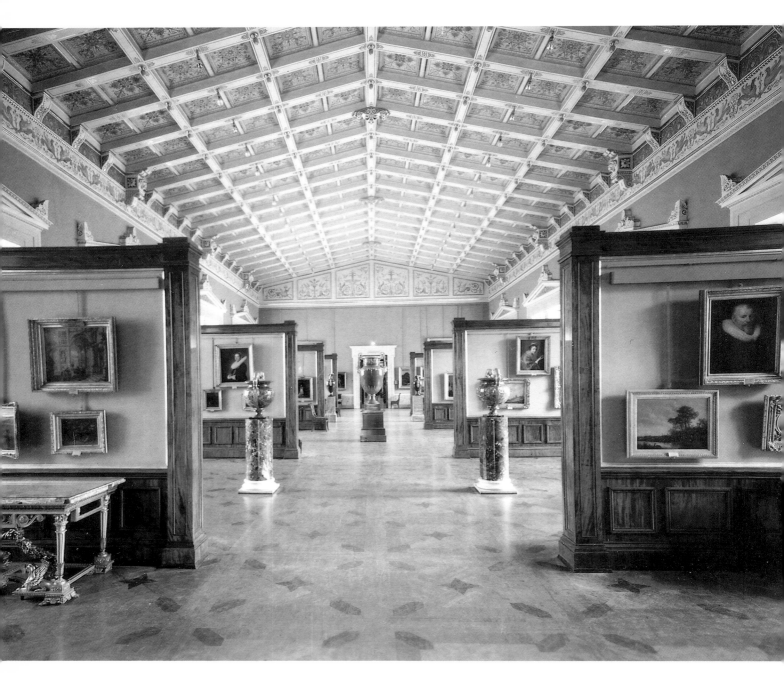

Fig. 1   The Hermitage: Tent Hall

INTRODUCTION

The collection of seventeenth-century Dutch and Flemish masterpieces at the Hermitage is one of the treasures of the museum and enjoys a reputation as one of the most important collections of its kind in the world. Today it comprises more than 1,800 canvases, including works by Rembrandt van Rijn, Peter Paul Rubens, Anthony van Dyck, Frans Hals, and Jacob van Ruisdael. With rare exceptions—the Hermitage has no works by Johannes Vermeer, for example—the collection contains paintings by all the major artists of the Dutch Golden Age, with a number of these artists extensively represented. Practically all stages in the evolution of Dutch and Flemish art, with their various genres and local schools, are included in the collection. In particular, paintings by pupils of Rembrandt and from the studio of Rubens are seen with exceptional diversity. But side by side with these masterpieces there are also works of fine quality by lesser-known artists. An important feature of the collection is the exceptional condition of the paintings, which is due to the fact that most of them came into the gallery during the first half of the eighteenth century, did not later change hands, and were thus not subjected to repeated restoration. In many ways the collection reflects the artistic tastes of the periods during which it was formed, as well as the personal tastes of those who assembled it. The present exhibition comprises a number of the most famous masterpieces in the Hermitage, including six works by Rembrandt and five by Rubens, spanning different stages in their artistic careers.

A few words about the gallery itself are in order. Although the collection is generally said to have been founded in 1764, when 225 canvases bought from the Berlin merchant I. E. Gotzkovsky arrived in Saint Petersburg, it includes several examples of Dutch and Flemish painting acquired at an earlier date, during the reign of Peter the Great (r. 1682–1725). The Russian czar's deep interest in Holland is well known. During his first tour abroad, in 1696, and on his second visit to Holland, in 1718, he often attended art auctions. According to his biographer Jacob Stoehlin von Storcksburg, Peter's favorite artists were Rembrandt, Rubens, Jan van Eyck, Jan Steen, Philips Wouwerman, Pieter Brueghel, Pieter van der Werff, and Adriaen van Ostade. In the early eighteenth century the czar's emissaries Yuri Kologrivov and Osip Solovev bought some 280 paintings at sales in The Hague, Amsterdam, Antwerp, and Brussels for the newly built palace of

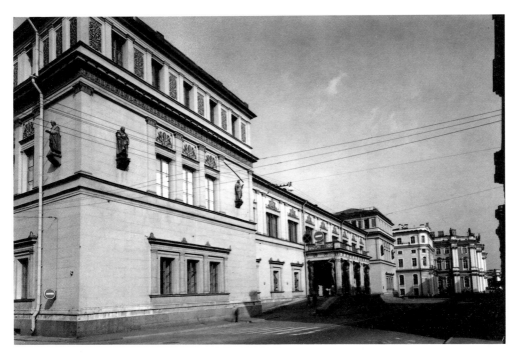

Fig. 2   The Hermitage. Built by Vasily Stasov and Nickolai Yefimov
after Leo von Klenze's design, 1842–51

Monplaisir at Peterhof. Of particular note among these works, which included paintings by Steen, Simon de Vlieger, Jacob Ochtervelt, and Jan Fyt, is Rembrandt's *David's Farewell to Jonathan*, the first work by this master to arrive in Russia. Purchased at an auction of Jan van Beuningen's collection held in Amsterdam on May 13, 1716, the canvas was valued at only 80 florins, while a work by Gerard de Lairesse was sold at the same auction for 12,000 florins. Another work bought during Peter's reign, Fyt's still life *Hare, Fruit, and Parrot*, is included in the present exhibition (no. 41).

The collecting of Dutch and Flemish paintings in Russia proceeded at a brisk pace. As early as the 1750s picture galleries in the palaces of Oranienbaum and Tsarskoye Selo were filled predominantly with Netherlandish paintings, some of which have ended up in the Hermitage. But the actual shaping of the collection and the establishment of an artistic standard took place from the 1760s to the 1780s. Shortly after coming to the throne in 1762, Empress Catherine II set about realizing her plans to create a court gallery that would rival the collections of Western Europe. The acquisitions she made over a period of twenty years remain the nucleus of the Hermitage's collection of masterpieces. The era began with the purchase of 225 paintings from I. E. Gotzkovsky in payment of a debt to the Russian state. The collection arrived in Saint Petersburg in the summer of 1764 and contained many works by Dutch and Flemish artists. Although the overall composition of the collection was mixed, it included a number of outstanding works, among them canvases by Rembrandt, van Dyck, Jacob Jordaens, Henrik Goltzius, and Abraham Bloemaert. It was from this collection too that Hals's *A Young Man Holding a Glove* (no. 11) was acquired. Another early acquisition made during Catherine's reign was van Ruisdael's *The Marsh* (no. 29), one of his most famous landscapes.

If the purchase of works from Gotzkovsky was rather arbitrary, subsequent acquisitions made in Western Europe demonstrated a purposeful and well-thought-out selection policy. In selecting paintings Catherine relied not only on her own tastes but also on the authoritative advice of experts—above all, the French encyclopedist Denis Diderot, the French sculptor Etienne-Maurice Falconet, and the German critic Melchior Grimm. Thanks to their support, in a remarkably short time both individual paintings and entire collections were bought at auction in Paris, at that time the most important art center in Europe. In the first years of the gallery's existence a major role in shaping the collection was played by Prince Dmitri Alekseyevich Golitsyn (1738–1803). This well-educated and gifted diplomat was an enthusiastic follower of the ideas of Diderot and Voltaire, and he combined the talents of a man of letters, a historian, and a natural scientist. From 1754 to 1768 he was posted at the Russian embassy in Paris, and in 1768 he was named Russian ambassador to The Hague. Golitsyn selected paintings for the gallery with exceptional energy and taste. It was thanks to him that the Hermitage secured Rembrandt's *Return of the Prodigal Son*. Two works in the present exhibition, Rembrandt's *Flora* (no. 22) and van Dyck's *Family Portrait* (no. 37), were also bought through his mediation. The former painting was included in a sale of Herman Arents's collection in Amsterdam in April 1770, while the latter was in the Paris collection of La Live de Jully. Appropriately enough, Prince Golitsyn also played a prominent role in establishing diplomatic contacts between Russia and the United States of America, after the latter country declared its independence in 1776. In 1789 he participated in the first direct diplomatic exchange between Russia and the United States, and his son, Dmitri Dmitrievich Golitsyn, lived in America for many years as a missionary under the name of Father Smith.

The first purchases for the gallery were made in Paris in 1766–68, when two collections were bought. One belonged to the portraitist J. A. J. Aved, and the other to the connoisseur Jean de Jullienne, a friend of Jean-Antoine Watteau. It was from this latter collection that Gabriel Metsu's *The Doctor's Visit* (no. 18) was acquired. But the most valuable purchases—those that were to be decisive for the formation of the Dutch and Flemish sections at the Hermitage—were from three other collections. The most important (1769) was that of Count Heinrich Brühl, the minister of August III of Saxony. The collection of Count Karl Cobentzl, minister to the Austrian court, was purchased in 1768. And in 1773 a number of works from the renowned picture gallery of Pierre Crozat in Paris were acquired.

In addition to the enormous collection of drawings (4,000 sheets) that now forms the basis of the Hermitage's Drawings Department, Count Cobentzl's collection contained forty-six paintings. Though small in number, it included such brilliant works as Rubens's *A Statue of Ceres in a Niche, Portrait of Charles de Longueval, Roman Charity* (no. 45), and *Venus and Adonis.*

Count Brühl's collection, on the other hand, comprised about 600 paintings, most of them by Dutch masters. The Hermitage bought three works by Frans van Mieris the Elder, four by Gerard ter Borch, five by van Ostade, numerous works by Wouwerman (a painter highly esteemed in the eighteenth century), and a magnificent selection of Italianate landscapes by Nicolaes Berchem, Jan Asselijn, and Adam Pynacker. Of particular significance, however, were four canvases by Rembrandt (one of them the *Portrait of a Scholar*, no. 23) and landscapes by van Ruisdael, whose *Waterfall in Norway* is included in the present exhibition (no. 30). The Flemish section contained works by Paul Bril, David Teniers, and David Ryckaert and two masterworks by Rubens, *Landscape with a Rainbow* and *Perseus and Andromeda.* The Brühl collection was also the source of Jan Brueghel I's *Village Street* (no. 36) and the earliest Rubens in the Hermitage collection, *The Adoration of the Shepherds* (no. 44).

The collection assembled by the Paris financier Pierre Crozat (1661–1740) was bought through the active intervention of Diderot and the Geneva collector François Tronchin. One of the collector's heirs—his nephew Louis-Antoine Crozat, Baron de Thiers and Marquis de Mois—had added to his share of the inheritance with his own acquisitions. By the end of his life he possessed 427 paintings of various schools, a huge library, and fine collections of sculpture and engravings. Since there was no male heir to continue the line, Crozat decided in his later years to part with these treasures. The purchase of his collection in 1772 enriched

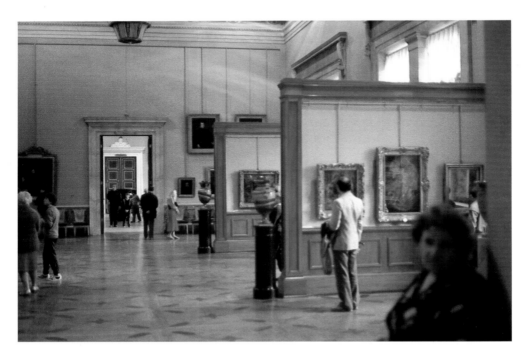

Fig. 3   The Hermitage: Dutch and Flemish galleries. Photo: James N. Wood

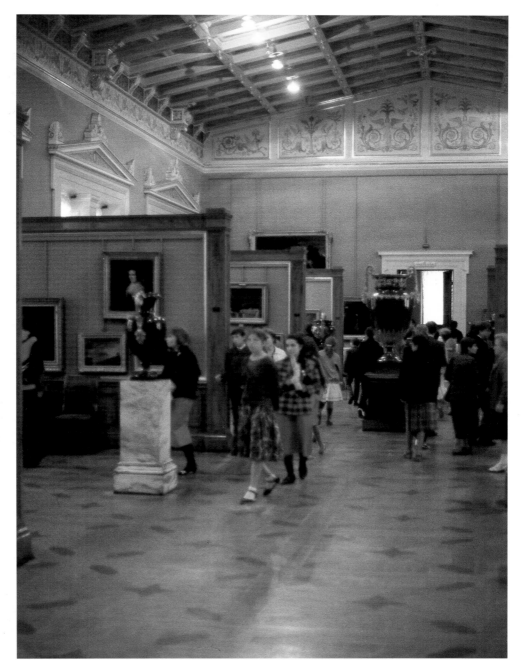

Fig. 4   The Hermitage: Tent Hall. Photo: James N. Wood

the Hermitage immeasurably. All the sections—Italian, French, Dutch, and Flemish—contained paintings of rare quality. From this collection came the *Portrait of a Lady's Maid*, *The Dismissal of Hagar*, *Bacchus*, and five oil sketches, all by Rubens, and five portraits by van Dyck (his *Self-portrait* is in the present exhibition; no. 39). Prominent among the Dutch paintings were works by Rembrandt, especially his *Danaë* and *The Holy Family* (no. 25).

In addition to the Crozat collection, other acquisitions, more modest in number but nonetheless extremely important, were made. In 1770 Prince Golitsyn informed Empress Catherine of an opportunity to buy the collection of François Tronchin, with whom he had engaged in a friendly correspondence. As a result the Hermitage added about a hundred paintings from various schools to its collections. For the most part these were smaller, more intimate works, such as Willem van de Velde's seascape *Ships in the Roads* (no. 32) and Emanuel de Witte's *A Protestant Gothic Church* (no. 33). Neither van de Velde nor de Witte had previously been represented in the Hermitage.

In 1774 the first printed catalogue of the collections was published. Totaling 2,080 entries, this catalogue marked the culmination of an important stage in the history of the museum. The creation of a major collection of paintings in Saint Petersburg—an enterprise about which even Diderot had been skeptical at first—had become a reality.

The Hermitage's Netherlandish holdings were further enriched by a number of important acquisitions made during the 1770s. Among the smaller collections purchased was that of the English collector John Blackwood in 1771. Of the forty-three works in this collection, the finest was Rembrandt's tragic and mysterious *Haman Recognizes His Fate (David and Uriah?)* (no. 26).

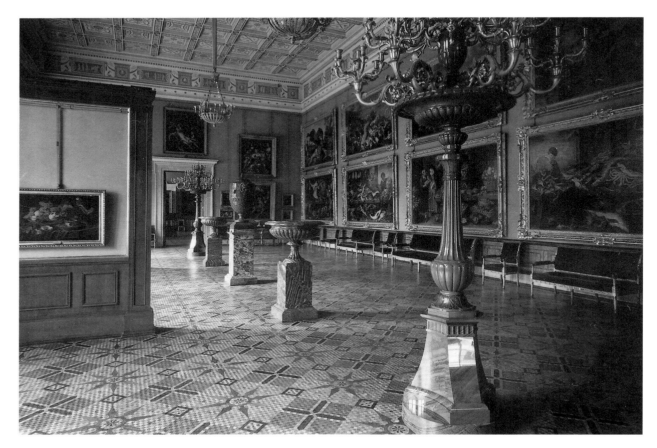

Fig. 5   The Hermitage: Dutch and Flemish galleries

Crucial purchases during this period included the collection of the British statesman Sir Robert Walpole, comprising 198 works, acquired in 1779, and the Baudouin collection, 119 works, bought in Paris in 1781. Walpole, who had served as prime minister to both George I and George II, kept his paintings at Houghton Hall, his family seat, and his gallery was reputed to house one of the finest private collections in England. The Walpole holdings included eight small oil sketches by Rubens; the *Madonna with Partridges* and ten portraits by van Dyck; a self-portrait by Jordaens; and four large still lifes by Frans Snyders. In addition to these works there were Rubens's *Landscape with Stone Carriers* (no. 46) and his sketches of *The Arch of Ferdinand* and *The Arch of Hercules* (nos. 47 and 48), the latter for the decoration of Antwerp on the occasion of Cardinal-Infante Ferdinand's visit in 1635; van Dyck's *Henry Danvers, Earl of Danby* (no. 40); and a single work by Rembrandt, *The Sacrifice of Isaac* (no. 24).

The Baudouin collection mainly supplemented the Dutch section of the Hermitage's holdings. It included nine works by Rembrandt (among them, *Portrait of an Old Jew*; no. 27) and numerous examples of Dutch landscape painting. Thus, by the end of the eighteenth century, the collections of Dutch and Flemish painting had for the most part taken their final form.

Some acquisitions for the gallery were also made in the Russian domestic

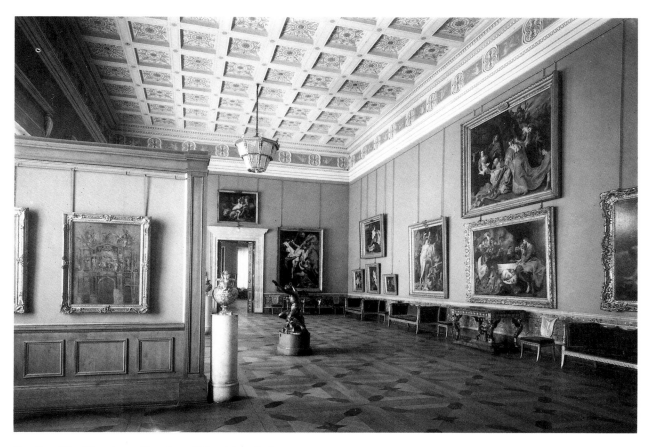

Fig. 6   The Hermitage: Dutch and Flemish galleries

market. The great private collections of such Russian aristocrats as I. I. Shuvalov, Prince A. M. Beloselsky, and Chancellor Prince A. A. Bezborodko were formed during the latter half of the eighteenth century. In 1763 the Imperial Academy of Arts in Saint Petersburg acquired a self-portrait by Michael Sweerts (no. 50) from the collection of I. I. Shuvalov. In the same year *The Dairymaid* (no. 7), an early work by Aelbert Cuyp in the possession of Prince G. A. Potemkin-Tavrichesky, was bought by Catherine II, along with other paintings from this collector's heirs.

Neither in scale nor in scope can the acquisitions made in the nineteenth century compare with those made during the reign of Catherine II, although the collection continued to grow at a remarkable rate. The most important additions of this period were the thirty-eight paintings that Emperor Alexander I bought from the Malmaison gallery of Napoleon's wife, Josephine, in 1814. Exemplary of the high quality of the Malmaison collection are ter Borch's *A Glass of Lemonade* (no. 4), Paulus Potter's *The Watchdog* (no. 21), and Teniers's *Monkeys in a Kitchen* (no. 51). The Hermitage's finest works by Potter were acquired with this collection, including his famous *The Farm.*

The Hermitage obtained a number of first-class Dutch paintings at the auction of works belonging to King Wilhelm II, held in 1850 at The Hague. Most of these paintings, however, had little impact on the collection as a whole, and the real significance of this period was the Hermitage's gradual transition from court gallery to museum. The buildings adjoining the Winter Palace that Catherine had had constructed to house her works—the Small Hermitage (1765–75, designed by the architects Felten and Delamot) and the Old Hermitage (1771–87, designed by Felten)—could no longer accommodate the rapidly expanding collections. The New Hermitage, designed by the German architect Leo von Klenze and constructed between 1840 and 1849, contained special exhibition galleries. On the second floor of this building, masterpieces of Dutch and Flemish painting were shown.

Toward the middle of the nineteenth century the first attempts were made to study the collection in a scholarly way. In 1864 a book by the noted authority Gustav Waagen was published; it was followed in 1873 by Wilhelm von Bode's study on the Dutch paintings in the Hermitage. In the latter part of the century the catalogues of the Dutch and Flemish collections went through several editions.

The long process of amassing the Netherlandish collection reached its culmination in the early years of the twentieth century. In 1910 more than 700 paintings by Dutch and Flemish artists were purchased from the collection of Petr Semenov-Tianshansky (1827–1915). This prominent explorer, civil servant, and scholar, who was the author of definitive works on geography, geology, entomology, botany, and statistics, had a passion for collecting, and he pursued it in a scientific and single-minded way. In buying the works of Dutch and Flemish masters over the course of half a century throughout Western Europe and Russia, Semenov-Tianshansky took into account the gaps that existed in the Hermitage's collections. By consulting such major experts as Bode and Bredius, he amassed a remarkable collection that included, in addition to works by famous masters, canvases by lesser-known artists. With the acquisition of his collection the names of 190 artists were added to the Hermitage's catalogue.

After the Revolution of 1917 many private collections owned by the Russian nobility were nationalized and their contents added to the Hermitage. Among these works were Hendrik ter Brugghen's *The Concert*, from the collection of Count V. N. Argutinsky-Dolgorukov (no. 6); a self-portrait by Samuel van Hoogstraten formerly in the Anichkov Palace (no. 13); and van Dyck's *Nicolaes Rockox*, formerly in the collection of Count Stroganov (no. 38). In 1922 the contents of the gallery of the Academy of Arts, the nucleus of which was the collection that Count N. A. Kushelev-Bezborodko had bequeathed to the Academy in 1862, were added to the Hermitage collections. Of particular note in this group are ter Borch's *Catrina van Luenink* (no. 3) and the monumental *Italian Landscape* by Jan Both (no. 5). Subsequent acquisitions were made through a specially appointed State Purchasing Commission, formed in 1935. Today private collections remain the primary source for the museum's holdings. In recent years the Hermitage has bought from private individuals works by Berchem, Both, Bloemaert, and Roelant Savery.

The Hermitage has experienced many dramatic episodes in its history. Twice —during World War I and World War II—the gallery's collections had to be evacuated; they were preserved only through the heroic efforts of its curators.

Irina Sokolova
Curator
The Hermitage

Note to the Reader

The catalogue entries were written by the following members of the curatorial staff of the Hermitage:

NB	N. Babina	KS	K. Semenova
NG	N. Gritsai	IS	I. Sokolova
IL	I. Linnik		

The research editors at the Hermitage were I. Linnik and K. Semenova.

The entries are in alphabetical order according to the artists' names.

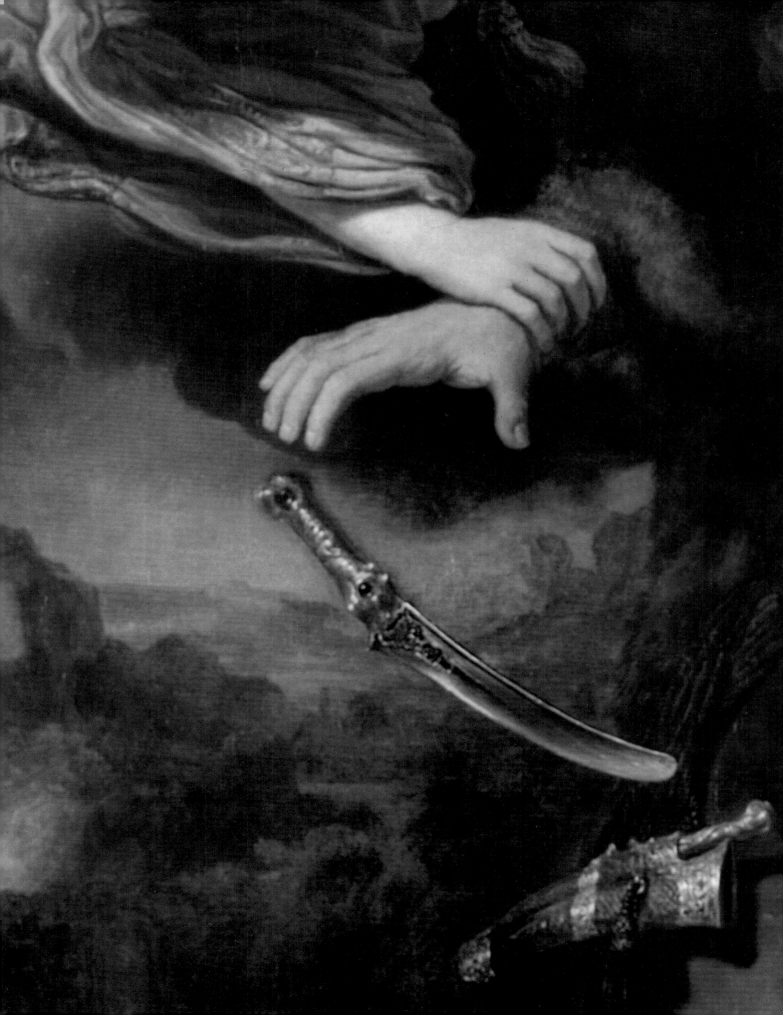

DUTCH PAINTINGS
OF THE
SEVENTEENTH
CENTURY

GERRIT BERCKHEYDE

1638 Haarlem–1698 Haarlem
Probably studied with his older brother Job Berckheyde. Worked in Haarlem
and from 1660 was a member of the painters' guild. Made a long journey
with his brother along the Rhine, visiting Cologne and Heidelberg (1650–53).
Painted townscapes, church interiors, and, to a lesser extent, genre scenes.

1. *The Departure for the Hunt*
    Oil on canvas, 20⅞ × 24⅝ in. (53 × 62.5 cm.)
    Signed lower left corner: Gerit Berck/Heyde
    Inv. no. 959

This painting draws on impressions and possibly sketches from the artist's
travels in Germany. Berckheyde is known to have used his drawings of German cities as the source for architectural motifs in the paintings he did after his
return home. The model for the building depicted here is probably the
Stapelhaus, a fifteenth-century castle in Cologne, though the image is far from
a literal rendition. Berckheyde would often place an actual architectural
motif in an imaginary setting or assemble monuments from a number of
different towns in a single composition. A variation on the Hermitage painting,
The Return from the Hunt (Willem Russell collection, Amsterdam), shows several interesting differences in the treatment of the castle. The themes of departure for and return from the hunt occur in a number of paintings by Berckheyde.
In his biography of the artist Arnold Houbraken recounts that in Heidelberg
Gerrit and his brother Job often watched the Elector and his suite departing
for the hunt and made this the subject of a painting that brought them considerable acclaim.

The sunlight, bright coloring, and transparent shadows, as well as the
figure of a girl carrying a basket of vegetables on her head, demonstrate the
painter's familiarity with works of the Italianate school.

PROVENANCE: Entered the Hermitage
between 1763 and 1774
HERMITAGE CATALOGUES: 1774, no. 1947;
1863–1916, no. 1215; 1958, II, p. 135; 1981,
p. 101

EXHIBITIONS: 1974 Le Havre, no. 1
LITERATURE: Waagen 1864, p. 255; Bode
1873; Fechner 1979, p. 42; Sokolova 1985,
p. 68

IS

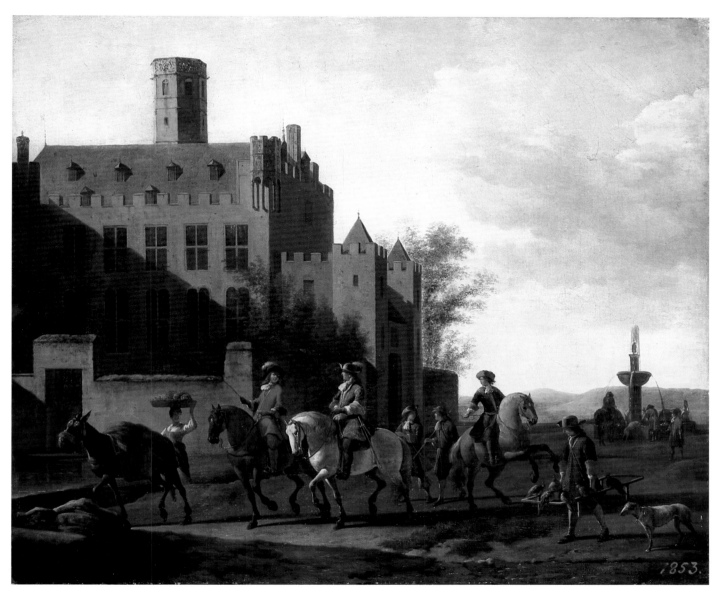

1

ABRAHAM BLOEMAERT

1564 Gorinchem–1651 Utrecht
Painter, draftsman, and engraver. Studied with his father, the architect
and sculptor Cornelis Bloemaert, and with Joost de Beer and Antonie
van Blocklandt in Utrecht. Lived in Paris (1580–83) and worked in Amsterdam
(1591–92) and Utrecht (from 1593).

2. *Landscape with the Prophet Elijah in the Desert*
Oil on canvas, 28⅜ × 37¼ in. (72 × 97 cm.)
Signed lower left: Bloemaert fecit.
Inv. no. 6802

Bloemaert emerged as the leader of the Utrecht school in the first decade of
the seventeenth century. He was a multifaceted artist who painted religious,
mythological, and genre subjects, as well as landscapes and portraits. In his
landscapes he attempts to abandon the Mannerist scheme of three differently
colored zones of space and to move from a global, cosmic view of nature to a
more intimate and lyrical one. His paintings are sometimes small and include
motifs of everyday village life, such as the gate, fence, and little building in the
present painting. Yet he never entirely escaped the Mannerist legacy, and his
depictions of nature retain a darkened foreground, unnatural color schemes,
and mannered ornamental foliage. Bloemaert often incorporated biblical episodes into his scenes of country life; here he has drawn on 1 Kings 17:1–7.

Müller (1927) dates the landscape to the second decade of the seventeenth century, a date confirmed by comparison with a number of landscapes
engraved after Bloemaert by Boetius à Bolswert in 1614. They are similar in
their general composition, as well as in the tendency to simplification and a
more expansive approach to composition.

PROVENANCE: Returned to the Hermitage
in 1931 from the Pavlovsk Palace Museum.
Entered the Hermitage before 1797. In
a dispatch sent to London the British
ambassador to Holland, Sir Dudley Carlton,
mentions the sale at auction on July 4, 1616,
of a painting by Abraham Bloemaert on the
same subject as the Hermitage work (*Oud
Holland*, 1985, p. 177). It is possible that the
work in question is the Hermitage painting.
In the sale catalogue of the Cornelis Sybilla
Roos collection, sold in Amsterdam on
November 24, 1806, no. 8 is described as
The Crows Feed Elijah in the Desert, a
painting by Abraham Bloemaert (40 × 50 in.
[101.6 × 127 cm.]). It is difficult to determine
if this was the Hermitage work.
HERMITAGE CATALOGUES: 1958, II, p. 139;
1981, p. 104
LITERATURE: Trubnikov 1912, p. 17;
Kharinova 1923, p. 89; Pappé 1926, p. 198;
Müller 1927, p. 208; Delbanco 1928, no. 17;
Fechner 1963, p. 167; Fechner 1971, pp. 111–17

IL

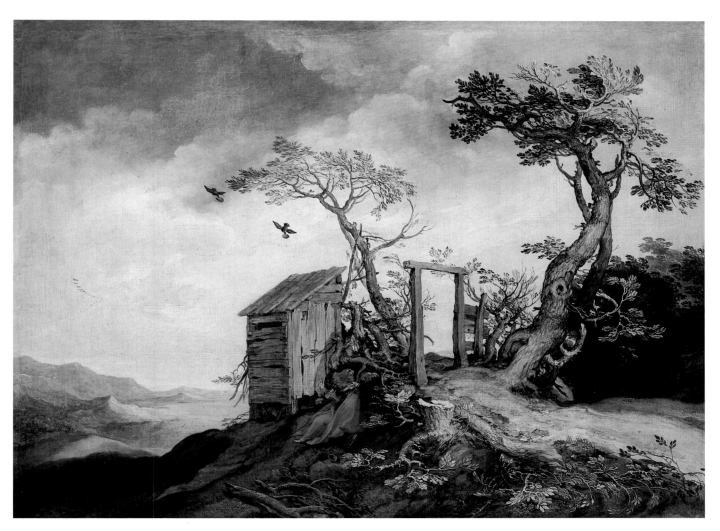

2

GERARD TER BORCH

1617 Zwolle–1681 Deventer
Studied with his father, Gerard ter Borch the Elder, and with Pieter
Molijn. Worked in Haarlem, Münster, Amsterdam, Zwolle, and Deventer.
Painted genre scenes and portraits.

3. *Catrina van Luenink*
    Oil on canvas, 31½ × 23¼ in. (80 × 59 cm.)
    Inv. no. 3783

The exquisite refinement found in many of ter Borch's works is even more
evident in his portraits, with their elegantly slender figures placed in calm,
natural poses and their noble bearing and gracefully restrained gestures. In
Catrina van Luenink ter Borch uses the most subtle gradations of whites, grays,
and blacks in an outstanding display of virtuoso technique.

    The sitter's identity was established by Gudlaugsson (1959–60) from the coat
of arms on the back of the canvas. Catrina van Luenink (1635–1680) was the wife
of Jan van Suchtelen, the burgomaster of Deventer. Ter Borch painted members of van Suchtelen's family on more than one occasion. The composition of
the Hermitage portrait suggests that there was a companion portrait of van
Suchtelen himself whose whereabouts is now unknown. Gudlaugsson believes
that the Hermitage portrait was the first in a series of female portraits executed
from the early 1660s on. Judging from the costume and the sitter's age, the
portrait was painted in 1662–63.

PROVENANCE: Transferred to the Hermitage
in 1922 from the Museum of the Academy
of Arts, Petrograd; formerly in the Kushelev
Gallery; prior to this in the collection of the
van Suchtelen family
HERMITAGE CATALOGUES: 1958, II, p. 279;
1981, p. 173

EXHIBITIONS: 1971 Tokyo–Kyoto, no. 46;
1975–76 Washington, D.C., no. 22; 1981
Madrid, p. 58; 1985 Rotterdam, no. 4
LITERATURE: Akademia Khudozhestv 1886,
no. 74; Hofstede de Groot 1912, V, no. 407;
Pappé 1925, p. 47; Gudlaugsson 1959–60,
no. 184; Kuznetsov and Linnik 1982, pl. 52

KS

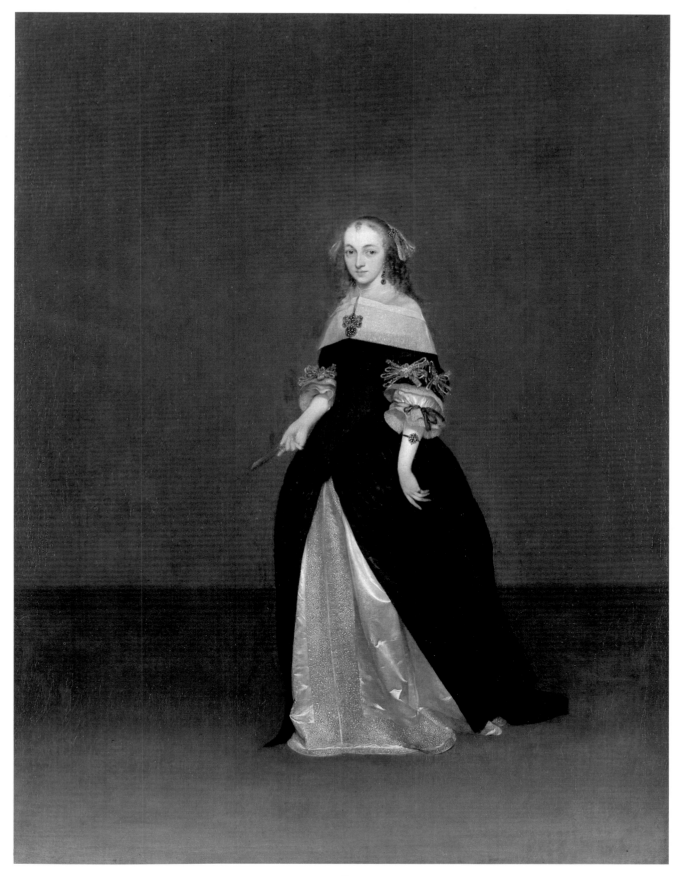

3

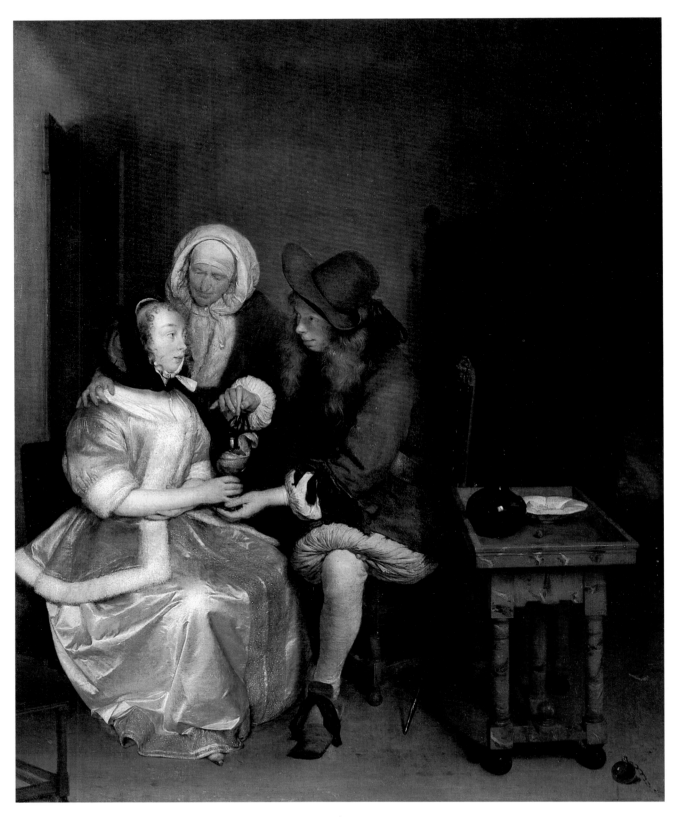

4

GERARD TER BORCH

4. *A Glass of Lemonade*
Oil on canvas, 26⅜ × 21¼ in. (67 × 54 cm.)
Inv. no. 881

Ter Borch's *A Glass of Lemonade*, with its soft chiaroscuro modeling, subtle color scheme, and masterful execution, is among the finest works of the Dutch school in the Hermitage. A brilliant painter, ter Borch combined great technical skill with a poetic approach to his subject matter. The lyrical mood that suffuses *A Glass of Lemonade* and the appearance of its protagonists, modeled on the painter's brother Moses and his sister Gesina, gave rise to a long-standing assumption that the painting depicts a scene in a family home. It is generally accepted now that the painting records a scene at the house of a procuress, a subject frequently encountered in Dutch art. This reading is borne out by the eloquent gesture of the old woman, who bares as if by chance the girl's shoulder, by the bed in the background, and by the significant glances exchanged by the young people.

A Glass of Lemonade was painted in the second half of the 1660s. An eighteenth-century engraving by A. L. Romanet (Choiseul collection, Paris) shows that at some point an anonymous artist added a lapdog on a chair (at left), a chandelier hanging from the ceiling (above), and a monkey chained to a metal ball (lower right). In the late eighteenth century these elements were removed, leaving only the ball with a length of chain.

PROVENANCE: Acquired by the Hermitage in 1814 from the collection of Empress Josephine at Malmaison; sold at the N. K. Hasselar auction held in Amsterdam, April 26, 1742 (no. 11); subsequently in the Gaignat collection in Paris in 1754; included in a sale of the Choiseul collection in Paris, April 6, 1774 (no. 25); sold at the Choiseul-Pralins auction in Paris, February 18, 1793 (no. 104), and then at the Choiseul-Pralins auction of May 18–19, 1808 (no. 18); later appeared at the de Séréville auction in Paris, January 22, 1812

HERMITAGE CATALOGUES: 1863–1916, no. 870; 1958, II, p. 281; 1981, p. 173
EXHIBITIONS: 1974 The Hague–Münster, no. 52; 1985 Rotterdam, p. 26, no. 3
LITERATURE: Livret 1838, XL, p. 35; Waagen 1864, p. 192; Neustroyev 1898, p. 258; Benois [1910], p. 345; Hofstede de Groot 1912, V, no. 87; Gudlaugsson 1948–49, pp. 235–67; Gudlaugsson 1960, no. 192; Kuznetsov and Linnik 1982, pls. 101, 102

KS

JAN BOTH

ca. 1615 Utrecht–1652 Utrecht
The year of his birth is not known; dates ranging from 1615 to
1620 appear in the literature. Studied with his father, Dirk Both,
and, according to Joachim von Sandrart (1675), with Abraham Bloemaert.
Worked in Rome (1638–41) and Utrecht (1641–52). Painted landscapes.

5. *Italian Landscape*
Oil on canvas, 60⅝ × 68½ in. (154 × 174 cm.)
Signed bottom left: JBoth f (J and B in ligature)
Inv. no. 3738

In this majestic canvas by a major Dutch contributor to the Italianate movement, an exceptional harmony has been achieved through the contrast of open
and closed spaces, of foreground and background, and of shapes in sunlight
and those in shadow. The groups of trees to left and right are wings through
which a river landscape is seen. The scene is suffused with a classical mood of
contemplative peace. The canvas probably dates from the later period of Both's
career, judging by such stylistic elements as the cool palette and the combination of broad brushwork with a detailed treatment of the leaves, grasses, and
flowers in the foreground. The large size of the painting is also significant, for
it was in the last years of his life that Both turned to such monumental landscapes.

PROVENANCE: Transferred to the Hermitage
in 1922 from the Museum of the Academy
of Arts, Petrograd, which it entered in 1862
as part of the N. A. Kushelev-Bezborodko
bequest
HERMITAGE CATALOGUES: 1958, II,
p. 143; 1981, p. 107

LITERATURE: Akademia Khudozhestv 1863,
no. 71; Waagen 1864, p. 422; Akademia
Khudozhestv 1868, no. 326; Akademia
Khudozhestv 1886, no. 8; Shcherbacheva
1924, p. 12; Pappé 1926, p. 200; Fechner
1963, pp. 120, 172, ill. 86; Kuznetsov and
Linnik 1982, pl. 214

IS

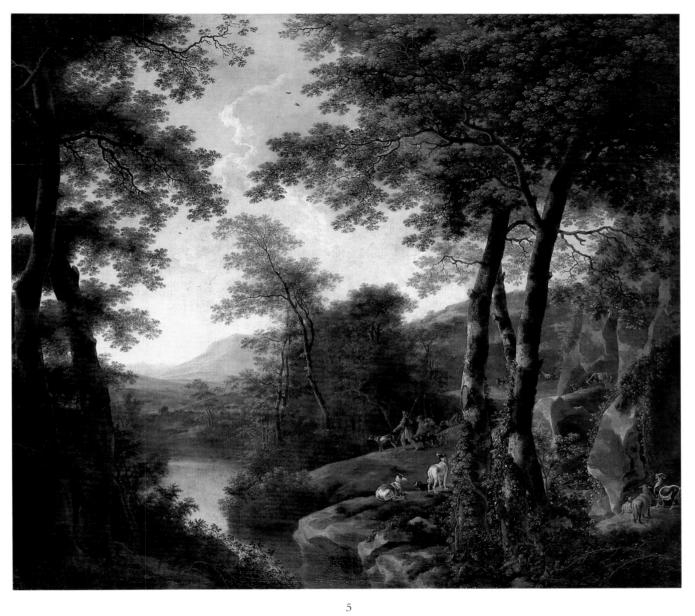

5

HENDRIK TER BRUGGHEN

1588 Deventer–1629 Utrecht
Studied with Abraham Bloemaert in Utrecht. Visited Italy (1604–16); was a
follower and perhaps a pupil of Caravaggio. Worked in Utrecht (from
1616/17 was a member of the painters' guild). Painted pictures on religious
and mythological themes and also genre scenes.

6. *The Concert*

Oil on canvas, 40¼ × 32⅝ in. (102 × 83 cm.)
Signed on sheet of music at right: HTB.1626.
Inv. no. 5599

Hendrik ter Brugghen's art has a distinctly national flavor. Although he spent
his youth in Italy he remained an artist of striking originality. In *The Concert*
the youthful fervor, the sweeping gestures, and the mischievous expressions of
the young musicians create an atmosphere of spontaneous merrymaking. Ter
Brugghen's specifically Dutch character can be seen in the types he depicts
—simple lads and lasses, broad-faced and perhaps a little coarse. It is in these
figures—without conventional prettiness but nonetheless extremely attractive
and likable—that ter Brugghen's great strength lies. His work is further distinguished by subtle painterly nuances, soft contours, and an austere palette.

Nicolson (1958) has noted a similarity between the Hermitage painting
and Gerrit van Honthorst's paintings *Concert* (1623; Statens Museum, Copen-
hagen) and *A Merry Company* (Alte Pinakothek, Munich).

A copy of this painting was previously in
the R. J. Sergejef collection, Geneva
(36¼ × 31⅛ in. [92 × 79 cm.]). A partial
copy, showing the figure of the violinist
but without the violin, was sold at the Jürg
Stuker auction, Bern, November 26–30,
1957, attributed to Honthorst (25¼ × 18⅞
in. [64 × 48 cm.])
PROVENANCE: Acquired by the Hermitage
in 1921 from the V. Argutinsky-Dolgorukov
collection, Petrograd

HERMITAGE CATALOGUES: 1958, II, p. 281;
1981, p. 173
EXHIBITIONS: 1956 Moscow–Leningrad,
p. 87; 1969 Leningrad, no. 75; 1972 Dresden,
no. 45; 1973 Leningrad, no. 60; 1977 Tokyo–
Kyoto, no. 17; 1981 Madrid, p. 60; 1985
Rotterdam, no. 6
LITERATURE: Nicolson 1958, no. 38;
Vsevolozhskaya and Linnik 1975, no. 12;
Nicolson 1979, p. 99; Zolotov 1979, p. 58

IL

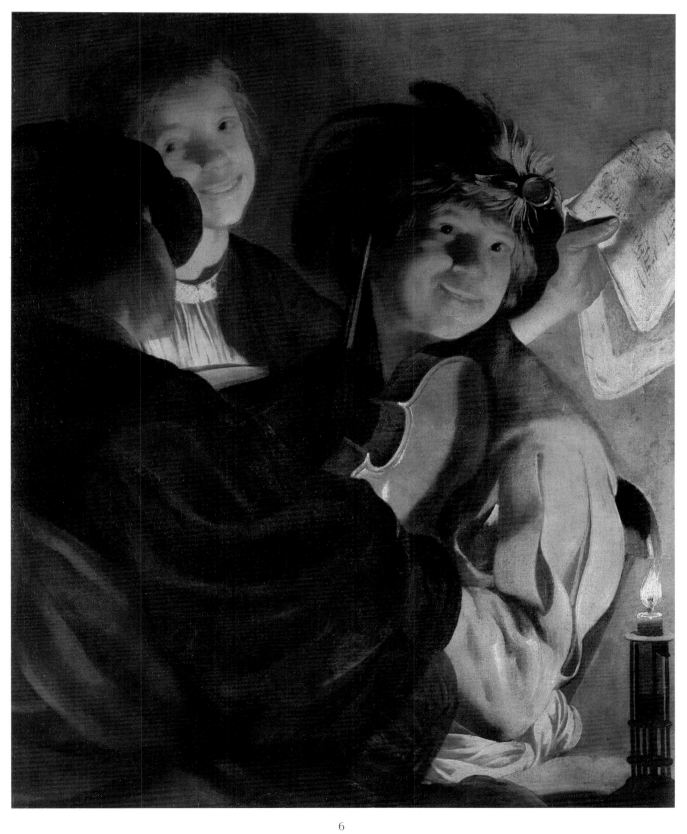

6

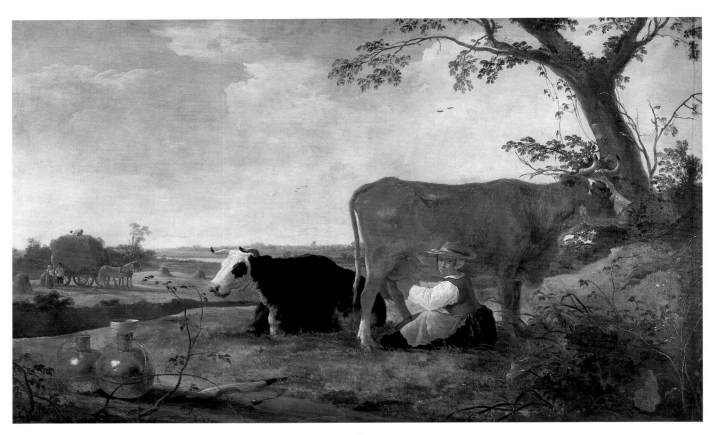

7

AELBERT CUYP

1620 Dordrecht–1691 Dordrecht
Born into a well-known family of Dordrecht painters. Studied with his father,
Jacob Gerritsz Cuyp. Two formative influences were Jan van Goyen and Jan
Both. Worked in Dordrecht; traveled throughout Holland. Landscape and
animal painter, occasional portraitist.

7. *The Dairymaid*
Oil on canvas, 41¾ × 67¾ in. (106 × 172 cm.)
Signed lower right: A Cuyp
Inv. no. 828

This painting can be dated on stylistic grounds to about 1647. Several known
works by Cuyp are variations on this broad, sunlit landscape with a young
dairymaid in the foreground. Unlike many of his contemporaries, who introduced staffage only to enliven a landscape, Cuyp gave animals and people an
important place in his paintings. The structure of this composition, the light
color range, and the figure of the peasant girl show lingering traces of the style
of the painter's father and teacher, Jacob Gerritsz Cuyp. A preparatory study of
the dairymaid was formerly in The Hague (reproduced in Reiss [1975]; present
location unknown). In the Rijksmuseum, Amsterdam, there is a sheet by Cuyp
depicting a recumbent cow, a motif found in the present painting.

VARIANTS: Duke of Sutherland collection; Weber collection, Hamburg, 1907 (Hofstede de Groot 1908, II, no. 367); National Gallery of Ireland, Dublin; Museum Boymans–van Beuningen, Rotterdam
PROVENANCE: Acquired by the Hermitage between 1794 and 1797; may have been in the Prince Potemkin-Tavrichesky collection, Saint Petersburg

HERMITAGE CATALOGUES: 1863–1916, no. 1107; 1958, II, p. 203; 1981, p. 136
LITERATURE: Livret 1838, p. 117, no. 31; Smith 1842, suppl., p. 649, no. 3; Waagen 1864, pp. 237–38; Bode 1873, p. 36; Neustroyev 1898, p. 295; Réau 1912, p. 483; Shcherbacheva 1924, p. 16; Reiss 1975, no. 57; Tarasov 1983, p. 145

IS

GERBRAND VAN DEN EECKOUT

1621 Amsterdam–1674 Amsterdam
Painter and etcher. Studied with Rembrandt (1635–40). Painted
historical subjects, portraits, and genre scenes.

8. *Abraham and Three Angels*
    Oil on canvas, 28 × 32¼ in. (71 × 82 cm.)
    Traces of signature and date at bottom left of bench leg:
        G. v. Eec . . . 1656
    Inv. no. 8523

Gerbrand van den Eeckout entered Rembrandt's studio at a very young age.
According to contemporary reports, he became his master's favorite pupil and
his friend. He was more gifted than his fellow pupils Ferdinand Bol and Govert
Flinck, although his achievements proved to be less important than theirs.
Abraham and Three Angels is based on Genesis 18:1–5. Its composition is
related to a work by Lastman (1616) in a private collection, but it has the
elegance characteristic of van den Eeckout's work.

There are two other paintings by the artist on this theme: one is in the
Rembrandtshuis, Amsterdam; the other, painted in 1672, was in an auction in
Frankfurt in 1897.

PROVENANCE: Acquired by the Hermitage
in 1938 through the Leningrad State
Purchasing Commission; formerly in the
Schidlovsky collection, Saint Petersburg
HERMITAGE CATALOGUES: 1958, II, p. 287;
1981, p. 187

EXHIBITIONS: 1956 Moscow–Leningrad,
p. 106; 1984 Warsaw, no. 6
LITERATURE: Sumowski 1983, no. 422

IL

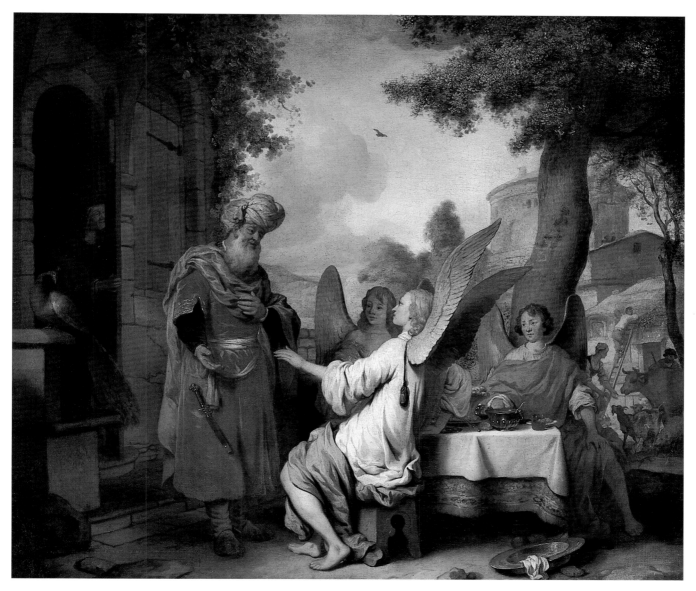

8

AERT DE GELDER

1645 Dordrecht–1727 Dordrecht
Studied with Samuel van Hoogstraten in Dordrecht and with Rembrandt
(early 1660s) in Amsterdam. Painted portraits and history pictures, more
rarely landscapes.

9. *Self-portrait*
   Oil on canvas, 31⅜ × 25½ in. (79.5 × 64.5 cm.)
   Signed right background: A. de Gelder: f.
   Inv. no. 790

Aert de Gelder was Rembrandt's last and most loyal pupil. He entered his
workshop at a period when the aging master had fallen out of fashion and had
few students. In this self-portrait of about 1710, de Gelder holds Rembrandt's
Hundred Guilder print, as if to stress his devotion to his teacher's memory. This
is all the more remarkable since it was painted at the end of the seventeenth
century, when idealizing trends reigned triumphant in Dutch art.

It is also significant not only that de Gelder remained faithful to Rembrandt's realism but that he tried to develop it still further by searching for the
psychological expressiveness of an image and by enriching his palette with new
and more delicate tones.

Several scholars have expressed doubts as to whether this is in fact a
self-portrait of de Gelder. However, as Sumovsky (1983) correctly pointed out,
this same figure appears at different ages in two other self-portraits by de
Gelder.

PROVENANCE: Acquired by the Hermitage in 1895 from Lazienski Palace, Warsaw; prior to this was sold to J. Eifer at the Jan van der Marck auction in Amsterdam, August 8, 1773 (no. 411)
HERMITAGE CATALOGUES: 1916, no. 831; 1958, II, p. 177; 1981, p. 126
EXHIBITIONS: 1956 Moscow–Leningrad, p. 74; 1972 Leningrad, no. 323; 1985 Rotterdam, no. 7
LITERATURE: Kramm, 1857–64, I, p. 556; Lacroix 1856–65, VIII, p. 54, no. 102; Moes 1897, I, no. 2669; Lilienfeld 1914, pp. 107, 114, no. 163; Sumovsky 1983, no. 811; Raupp 1984, p. 348.

IL

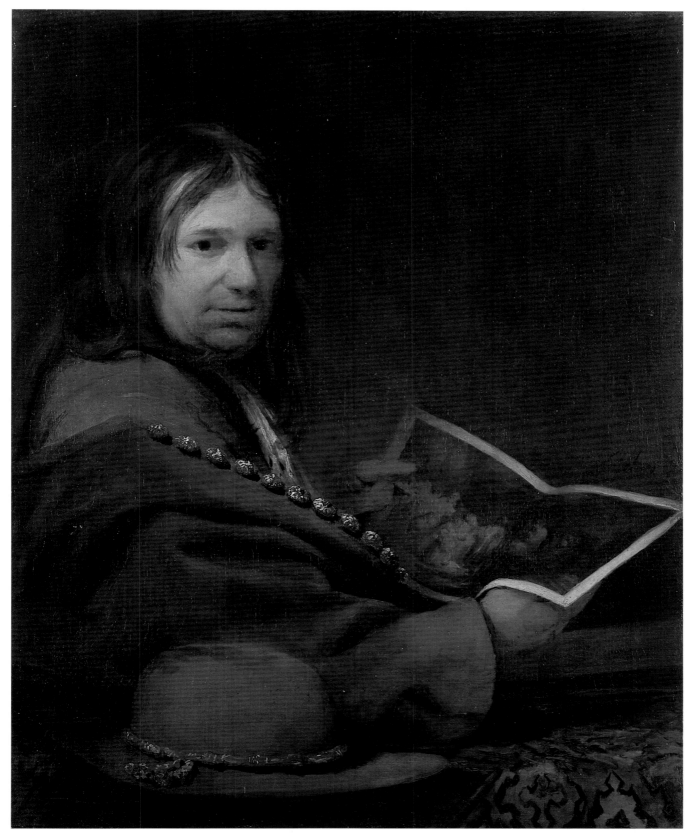

9

JAN VAN GOYEN

1596 Leiden–1656 The Hague
Studied with Isaac van Swanenburgh in Leiden, Willem Gerritsz in Hoorn, and most importantly with Esaias van de Velde in Haarlem. Spent time in France (ca. 1615), Flanders (1615), and Germany and traveled extensively in his own country. Worked in Haarlem (1615–17 and 1634), Leiden (until 1631), and The Hague (1631–56). One of the creators and great masters of the monochrome landscape.

10. *Landscape with an Oak*
Oil on canvas, 34⅝ × 41⅜ in. (83 × 105 cm.)
Signed and dated at right: VGOYEN 1634 (V and G in ligature)
Inv. no. 806

This painting's central motif, an old oak with dead branches and a twisted trunk, appears in a number of paintings by van Goyen from the 1630s to the early 1640s. Among the artist's drawings are several studies of a tree, of which the closest to the Hermitage painting is a drawing in the collection of Dr. Lisa Oehler, Kassel (Beck 1972–73, I, no. 133). According to Romanov (1936), this motif is iconographically linked to Gerard Segher's engraving *Old Oak Tree and Distant View* (Hollstein, XXVI, p. 207, no. 28). It should be pointed out that about 1600 a single tree with fantastically twisted branches was a recurring motif in the work of Dutch artists (notably Hendrik Goltzius, Abraham Bloemaert, and Jacques de Gheyn the Elder). But whereas these older artists were attracted by the tense, fantastic forms of the trunk and branches broken by stormy weather, van Goyen minimizes the oak's dramatic aspect and makes the tree just another characteristic feature of the humble country landscape.

The two riders conversing with pilgrims at the left depend from a drawing dated 1634 (art market, Vienna, 1969). This same genre scene was later used by van Goyen's pupils.

PROVENANCE: Transferred in 1920 to the Hermitage from Gatchina Palace, where it had been since the early nineteenth century
HERMITAGE CATALOGUES: 1958, II, p. 183; 1981, p. 127
EXHIBITIONS: 1908 Saint Petersburg, no. 455; 1968–69 Belgrade, no. 30; 1972 Leningrad, no. 26; 1981 Vienna, pp. 46–47; 1983 Tokyo, no. 8; 1985 Rotterdam, no. 8

LITERATURE: Shchavinsky 1916, p. 69; Hofstede de Groot 1923, VIII, no. 315; Shcherbacheva 1924, p. 8; Pappé 1926, p. 200; Volhard 1927, p. 174; Romanov 1936, p. 189; Waal 1941, p. 24; Fechner 1963, p. 30; Stechow 1966, p. 28, no. 38; Dobrzycka 1966, p. 38, no. 70; Beck 1972–73, II, no. 1132; Kuznetsov and Linnik 1982, pl. 185

IS

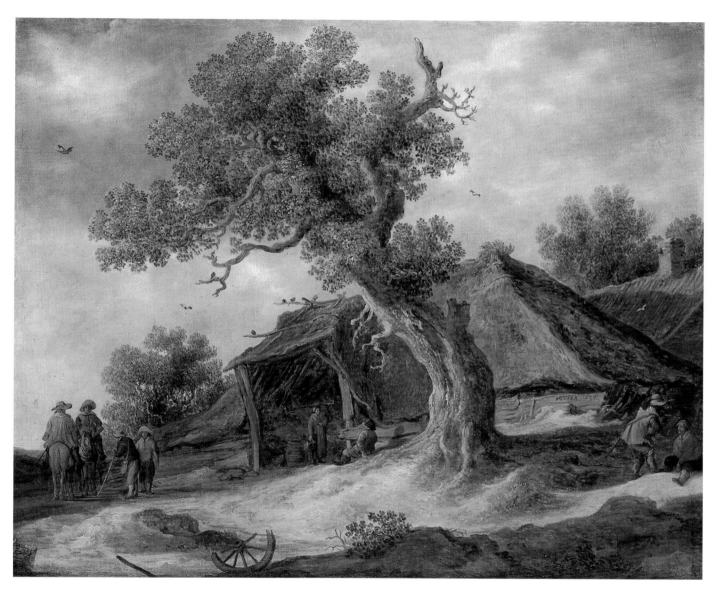

10

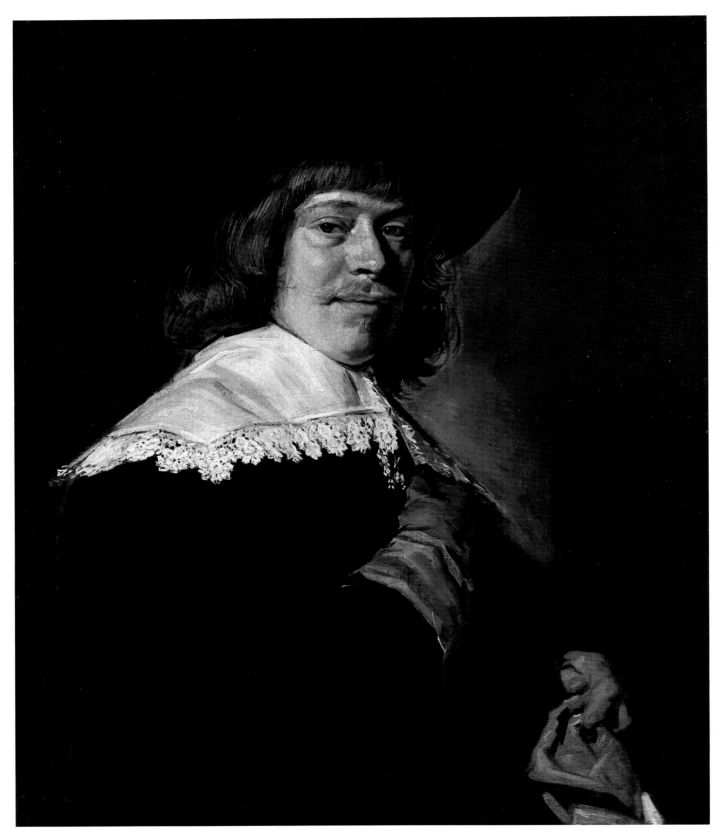

11

FRANS HALS

1581/85 Antwerp–1666 Haarlem
Studied with Carel van Mander in Haarlem. Worked in Haarlem.
Painted single and group portraits and genre subjects. Among his students
were Adriaen van Ostade, Adriaen Brouwer, Judith Leyster, and Jan Miense
Molenaer.

11. *A Young Man Holding a Glove*
Oil on canvas, 31½ × 26⅛ in. (80 × 66.5 cm.); strips added to
the sides and the upper edge. Monogram in right background:
FH; traces of a second monogram at left
Inv. no. 982

This portrait reflects the changes in Hals's work during the 1640s. The opti-
mism of his earlier period, with its hint of rebelliousness and democratic
challenge, has given way to greater restraint and composure; traces of weari-
ness and melancholy, sometimes irony and skepticism, have appeared. The
spontaneous poses of Hals's previous works have been replaced by a sense of
repose, and the palette resonates with cold silver blacks and olive-gray tones.

Slive (1970–74) has shown that the Hermitage portrait served as the model
for an engraving by E. le Devis, who combined it (in reverse) with the so-called
Mulatto (Museum der Bildenden Künste, Leipzig). The engraving was published in London about 1670 under the title *The Mountebank Doctor and His
Merry Andrew*. This combination is not surprising: the mountebank doctor and
his buffoon assistant would stage theatrical performances in the market square
to attract a crowd, then move on to selling their medicines and "physicking."

Slive correctly concludes that the combination of these two figures on a
single page would have been E. le Devis's idea, since Hals would not have united
a traditional portrait with a comic figure that, moreover, had been painted a
decade earlier. He further suggests that the sitter for the Hermitage portrait
could have been a real doctor and that at some point the portrait found its way
to England. In support of this theory Slive refers to one of G. Wertier's notebooks,
in which Wertier mentions a portrait of a doctor by Frans Hals in his possession
(signed with Hals's monogram), and to information provided by R. I. Hutchinson,
the curator of the Scottish National Portrait Gallery, Edinburgh, regarding the
appearance of a "fine portrait of a doctor by Francis Hals" at a sale of the
collection of Colonel Charteris about 1732 (no. 99). In both cases it is highly
probable that the work in question was the Hermitage portrait.

Bode (1883) dates the portrait to the 1640s, Hofstede de Groot (1910) to
1647, and Valentiner (1923) to 1645. Slive finds it close in style to Hals's
Portrait of a Man (Wallraf-Richartz-Museum, Cologne) and *Portrait of the
Regents of Saint Elizabeth's in Haarlem* (Frans Halsmuseum, Haarlem) and
dates it to about 1640.

PROVENANCE: Acquired by the Hermitage
in 1764 from the Gotskovsky collection,
Berlin; before this was possibly in England
ca. 1670
HERMITAGE CATALOGUES: 1797, no. 1239;
1863–1916, no. 771; 1958, II, p. 170; 1981,
p. 176
EXHIBITIONS: 1972 Moscow, pp. 59–60; 1977
Tokyo–Kyoto, no. 19

LITERATURE: Waagen 1864, no. 771; Bode
1883, p. 129; Moes 1909, p. 181; Hofstede
de Groot 1910, III, no. 308; Bode and Binder
1914, pl. 194; Valentiner 1923, p. 197; Trivas
1941, p. 76; Slive 1970–74, I, p. 97, II,
p. 214; III, p. 74, no. 134

KS

GERRIT VAN HONTHORST

ca. 1590 Utrecht–1656 Utrecht
Studied with Abraham Bloemaert in Utrecht. Worked in Rome (1610–19),
Utrecht (1620–30, 1652–56; from 1622 a member of the painters' guild),
London (1628), and The Hague (1635–52).

12. *Christ in the Garden of Gethsemane*
Oil on canvas, 44½ × 43¼ in. (113 × 110 cm.)
Inv. no. 4612

Gerrit van Honthorst was the most famous and prolific of the Dutch
Caravaggists, and in such early works as the present painting came closest to
Caravaggio's mature style. This painting demonstrates those qualities that won
Honthorst fame in Italy: the agitated energy with which he invests his narrative,
his mastery of chiaroscuro and composition, and his undoubted gifts as a colorist.
It was also in Italy that he was given the nickname Gerardo della Notte
(Gerard of the Night), because of his fondness for night scenes illuminated by
artificial light. The light in Honthorst's paintings not only emphasizes the mass
of things and creates an unusual compositional sharpness but also lends the
scene a peculiar intimacy and feeling.

The story of Christ in the Garden of Gethsemane occurs in all four Gospels,
but Honthorst's interpretation corresponds most closely to Luke (22:41–44),
which tells that an angel appeared to Christ as he prayed to "strengthen" him.

The painting was initially attributed to an anonymous seventeenth-
century Italian artist. The attribution to Honthorst was made by Shcherbacheva (1956) after comparison with the paintings *Madonna and Child with
Saint Francis of Assisi and Saint Bonaventure* (Albano monastery, near Rome)
and *The Adoration of the Angels* (Galleria degli Uffizi, Florence).

The author agrees with Judson (1959), who dated the Hermitage painting
to about 1617.

PROVENANCE: Acquired by the Hermitage
before 1859
HERMITAGE CATALOGUES: 1958, II, p. 186;
1981, p. 184
EXHIBITIONS: 1956 Moscow–Leningrad,
p. 96; 1973 Leningrad, no. 73; 1985
Rotterdam, no. 14

LITERATURE: Shcherbacheva 1956, I, pp.
118–21; Judson 1959, no. 39; Vsevolozhskaya
and Linnik 1975, nos. 95–97; Nicolson
1979, p. 58; Zolotov 1979, p. 56; Linnik
1980, p. 72; Kuznetsov and Linnik 1982,
pl. 120

IL

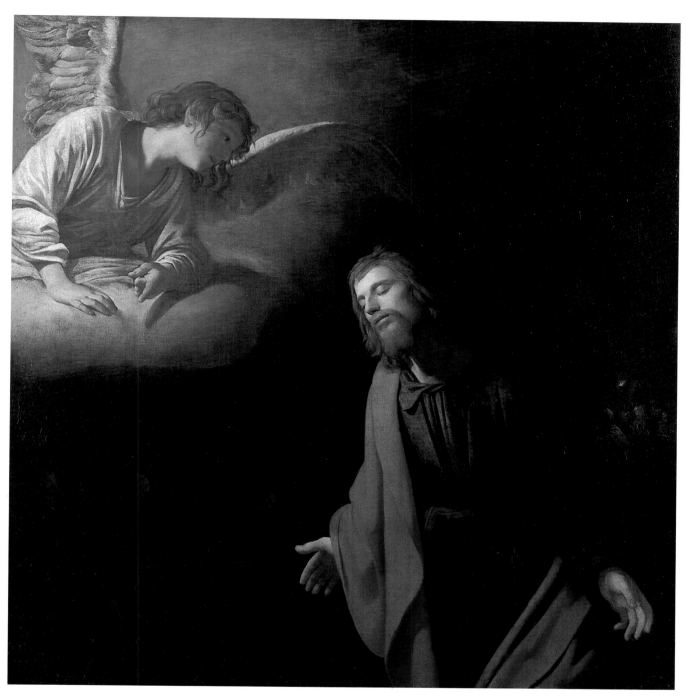

12

SAMUEL VAN HOOGSTRATEN

1627 Dordrecht–1672 Dordrecht
Studied with his father Dirk van Hoogstraten in Dordrecht and with Rembrandt in Amsterdam. Worked in Dordrecht (1648–51, 1654–62), London (1662–66), and The Hague (1668–71; from 1668 a member of the Pictura confraternity). Visited Vienna (1651) and Rome (1652). Painted genre scenes, religious and historical subjects, and portraits. Wrote on the history of art (his *Inleyding tot de Hooge Schoole der Schilderkonst*, published in Rotterdam in 1678, is particularly significant).

13. *Self-portrait*
Oil on canvas, 40⅛ × 31⅛ in. (102 × 79 cm.)
Inv. no. 788

Van Hoogstraten painted many self-portraits; the majority of them have long been known, but those in Soviet collections (the Hermitage and the Voronezh Museum of Art) have been identified only recently.

When it was acquired by the Hermitage the present self-portrait was attributed to Ferdinand Bol under the title *Portrait of an Artist*. It appeared as such in the 1958 catalogue of paintings in the Hermitage. The assumption that it is in fact a self-portrait by van Hoogstraten has been expressed by a number of scholars, including Bauch (1966). This opinion is shared by the present author.

PROVENANCE: Transferred to the Hermitage in 1918 from Anichkov Palace, Petrograd
HERMITAGE CATALOGUES: 1958, II, p. 142 (as Ferdinand Bol, *Portrait of an Artist*); 1981, p. 182 (as Hoogstraten [?], *Self-Portrait*)

EXHIBITIONS: 1985 Rotterdam, no. 16
LITERATURE: Pappé 1925, p. 154; Bauch 1966; Linnik 1980, p. 127; Blankert 1982, p. 173, no. R103

IL

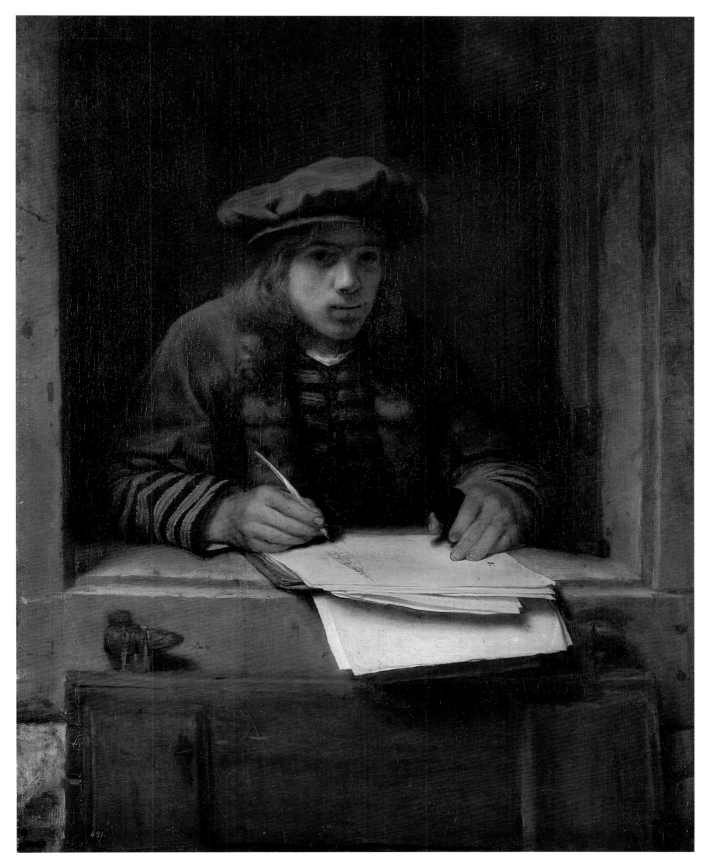

13

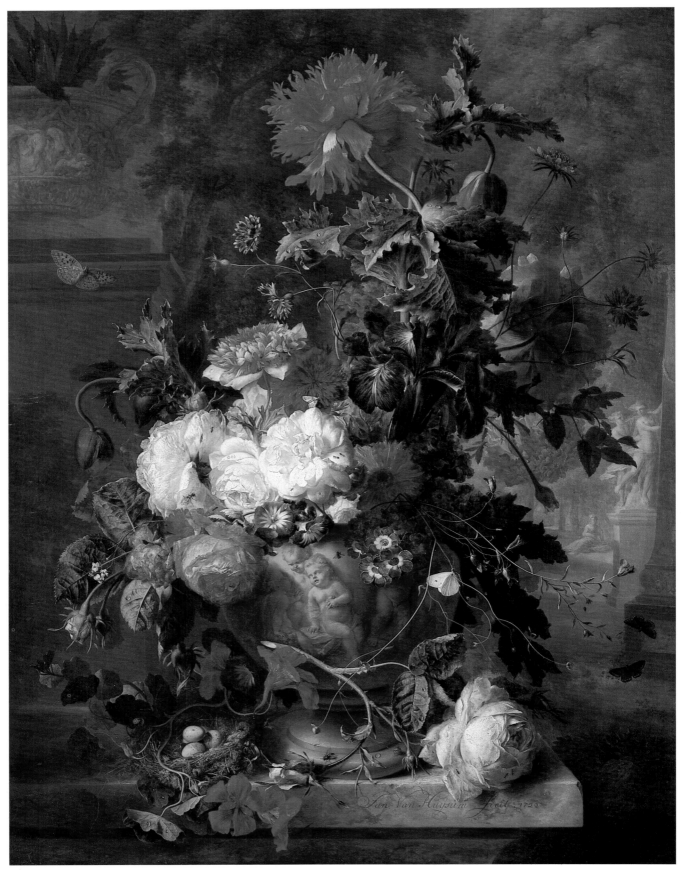

JAN VAN HUYSUM

1682 Amsterdam–1749 Amsterdam
Studied with his father, Joost van Huysum, a painter of decorative floral still lifes. Worked primarily in Amsterdam. Painted still lifes of flowers and fruits and also arcadian landscapes.

14. *A Bouquet of Flowers*
   Oil on canvas (transferred from wood in 1835), 31⅛ × 23⅝ in.
      (79 × 60 cm.)
   Signed and dated right corner: Jan Van Huysum fecit 1722
   Inv. no. 1051

This magnificent bouquet, composed of a variety of luxuriant seasonal blooms, stands in a vase on a stone pedestal. The flowers' structure, form, and coloring have been captured with stunning virtuosity. In contrast to the older generation of artists, Jan van Huysum is known to have painted his flowers from nature; the yellow rose at the lower right (*Rosa huysumiana*) was a particular favorite of his. The plant world also had a symbolic subtext: the butterflies (the personification of the human soul), insects, and torn, wilted rose are well-known emblems of *vanitas*, reminding the viewer how transitory is the blossoming of earthly things. The putti on the ceramic vase are also part of this moralizing tradition. In the distance there is a park landscape with a sculptural group modeled on Gianlorenzo Bernini's *Apollo and Daphne* (Galleria Borghese, Rome).

Huysum first used this type of composition—a bouquet of flowers shown against a light background—about 1720. The Hermitage painting is one of his most refined works. Together with its companion piece, *Flowers and Fruits* (Hermitage, inv. no. 1049), it entered the Walpole collection at Houghton Hall in the eighteenth century. The two paintings were seen and described by George Vertue, who noted that Walpole bought them for 300 francs. In the old Hermitage catalogues both paintings appear with the note "commissioned by . . . Walpole," but there is no documentary evidence to support this claim.

A mezzotint of the painting was made by Richard Earlom in 1778 (Le Blanc 1854–89, no. 53).

PROVENANCE: Acquired by the Hermitage in 1779 from the Walpole collection, Houghton Hall, England
HERMITAGE CATALOGUES: 1863–1916, no. 1379; 1958, II, p. 175; 1981, p. 178
EXHIBITIONS: 1983 Tokyo, no. 45
LITERATURE: Aedes Walpolianae 1752, p. 70; Aedes Walpolianae 1767, p. 70; Smith 1835, VI, no. 99; Livret 1838, p. 470, no. 22; Waagen 1864, p. 275; Bode 1873, p. 45; Neustroyev 1898, p. 311; Shcherbacheva 1926, pp. 47, 57; Hofstede de Groot 1928, X, no. 68; Vertue 1930, I, p. 80, note 7; Shcherbacheva 1945, pp. 57, 70; Grant 1954, no. 28; Vertue 1968, VI, p. 179; Fechner 1981, pp. 34, 172; Kuznetsov and Linnik 1982, pl. 286

IS

PIETER JANSSENS ELINGA

Brugge 1623–before 1682 Amsterdam(?)
Probably studied with his father, the painter Gisbrecht Janssens. Influenced by Pieter de Hooch. Worked in Rotterdam and Amsterdam. Painted genre scenes and still lifes.

15. *Room in a Dutch House*
Oil on canvas, 24¼ × 23¼ in. (61.5 × 59 cm.)
Inv. no. 1013

Janssens Elinga's art was directly influenced by the painting of Pieter de Hooch. Like de Hooch he devoted his career to glorifying the bourgeois way of life and the cult of home and hearth. In artistic terms he was most interested in the problems of depicting sunlight as it penetrates a room and capturing the light and the air that fill interior spaces.

Like most of Janssens Elinga's genre paintings, *Room in a Dutch House* was long attributed to Pieter de Hooch. Lipgart (1912) was the first to attribute it to Janssens. There are two variants of the Hermitage canvas: one is in the Musée du Petit Palais, Paris; the other was formerly in the Rickoff collection, Paris. Hofstede de Groot (1891) and Brière-Misme (1948) have suggested that *Room in a Dutch House* and *Woman Reading* (Alte Pinakothek, Munich) were conceived as companion pieces. Brière-Misme has also argued that the two paintings formed a diptych, with one canvas showing the active life and the other the contemplative life. However, neither of these hypotheses has been substantiated.

PROVENANCE: Acquired by the Hermitage in 1912 from the P. S. Stroganov collection, Saint Petersburg
HERMITAGE CATALOGUES: 1916, no. 1970 (as Pieter Janssens?); 1958, II, p. 288; 1981, p. 189

EXHIBITIONS: 1968–69 Belgrade, no. 37
LITERATURE: Waagen 1864, p. 412 (as Pieter de Hooch); Hofstede de Groot 1891, pp. 286–88; Lipgart 1912, p. 33; Brière-Misme 1948, pp. 347–54; Fechner 1979, pp. 39, 252; Sutton 1984, p. 203

KS

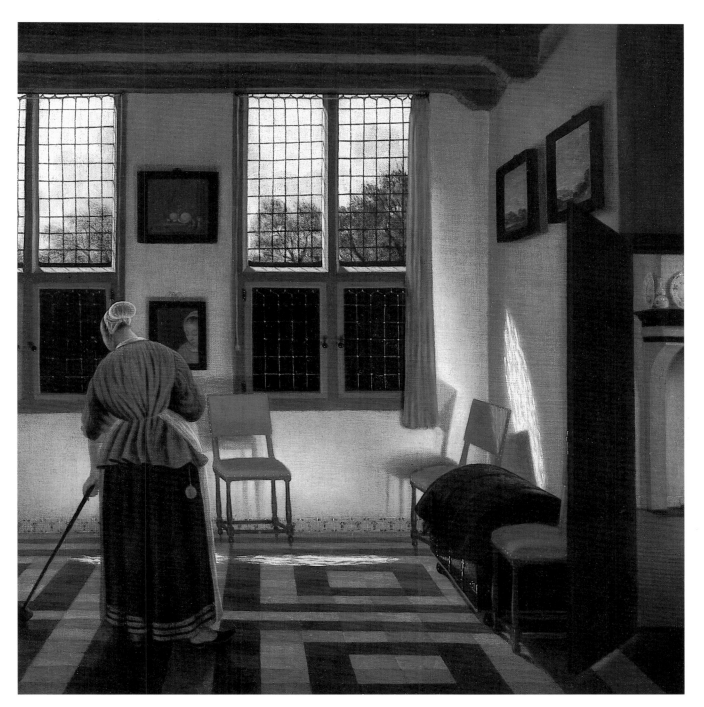

15

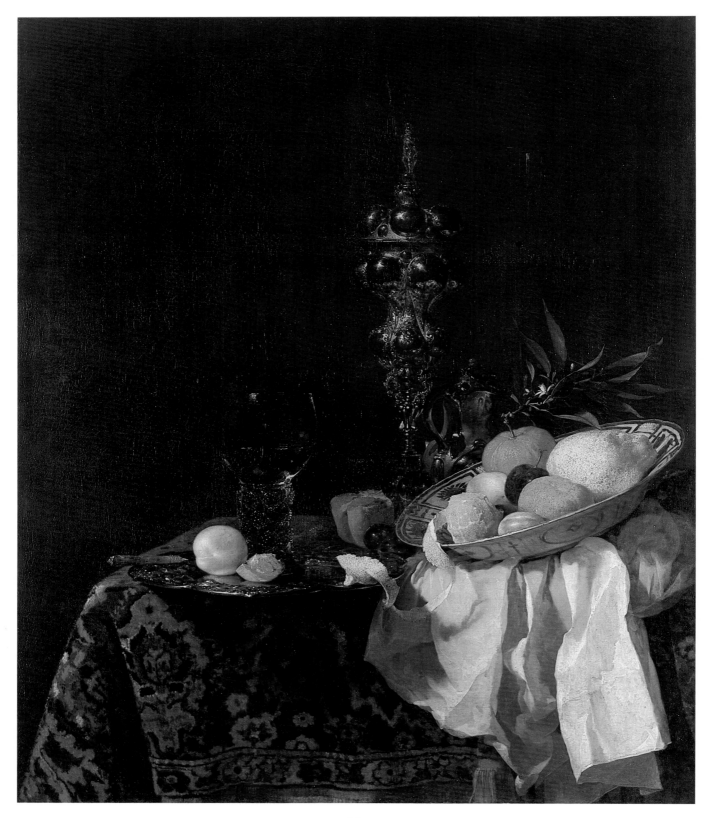

16

WILLEM KALF

1619 Rotterdam–1693 Amsterdam
Pupil of Hendrick Pot. Lived in Paris (1642–46) and possibly for a short
time in Italy. Worked in Amsterdam. Painted still lifes and small pictures
depicting peasant courtyards and kitchens.

16. *The Dessert*
    Oil on canvas, 41⅜ × 34½ in. (105 × 87.5 cm.)
    Signed lower left background: WKalf (W and K in ligature)
    Inv. no. 2822

This work was created between 1653 and 1664, when, under the influence of
the Amsterdam school and Rembrandt's later work in particular, Kalf produced his finest paintings. Like most of Kalf's still lifes from this period, the
present work is distinguished by its refinement and the care with which the
artist has selected his subjects—the costly dishes and ripe fruits arranged in a
pyramid on a table covered with a magnificent Persian carpet. The deep, warm
colors, unified by muted chiaroscuro, create an impression of sumptuousness
and nobility. The objects in the still life reappear in other paintings by Kalf: the
silver dish with the roemer, fruits, and knife recalls a still life in the T. H. Smidt
van Heller collection in Arnhem, while the same *akelpokal* (golden guild cup) is
depicted in several still lifes painted by Kalf about 1653–54.

PROVENANCE: Acquired by the Hermitage
in 1915 from the P. P. Semenov-Tianshansky
collection, Petrograd
HERMITAGE CATALOGUES: 1958, II, p. 198;
1981, p. 134
EXHIBITIONS: 1915 Petrograd, p. 25; 1972
Dresden, no. 86; 1984 Leningrad–Moscow,
no. 36; 1981 Madrid, p. 42; 1985 Rotterdam,
no. 17

LITERATURE: Semenov 1906, p. 150, no. 244;
Shchavinsky 1909, p. 259; Shcherbacheva
1945, pp. 52–53; Kuznetsov 1966, pp. 184,
185, no. 41; Grisebach 1974, p. 156, no. 79;
Fechner 1981, pp. 22, 25, nos. 45, 46;
Kuznetsov and Linnik 1982, pl. 264

KS

PIETER LASTMAN

1583 Amsterdam–1633 Amsterdam
Studied with Gerrit Pietersz Sweelinck and Cornelis Cornelisz van Haarlem.
Worked in Rome (1603–5); then returned to Amsterdam. Influenced by
Adam Elsheimer and Caravaggio.

17. *Abraham on the Road to Canaan*
    Oil on canvas (transferred from wood), 28⅜ × 48 in.
       (72 × 122 cm.)
    Signed and dated on stone at left: Pietro Lastman fecit A° 1614
    Inv. no. 8306

Rembrandt's teacher Pieter Lastman was a leading exponent of history painting, and his name is linked to the most important achievements in this genre
during the pre-Rembrandt period.

As early as the second decade of the seventeenth century, Lastman had
created a type of history painting new for his time. In 1614 he painted one of
his best works, *Abraham on the Road to Canaan* (Genesis 12:1–7, especially
verse 7, "And the Lord appeared to Abram, and said, 'Unto thy seed I will give
this land.'"). This biblical episode spoke directly to the Dutch people. In 1609
the United Provinces (Holland, Zeeland, Utrecht, Gelderland, Overijssel, Fries-
land, and Groningen) concluded a truce with Spain, ending a long struggle for
independence. Political speeches, verses by poets, and sermons expressed great
joy at the long-sought achievement of peace. Biblical metaphors were universally used—the Dutch were the Chosen People; like Abraham, they had a
covenant with God, who pledged that they would possess the Promised Land.
It is not surprising that Lastman expressed his own feelings in universally
understood biblical images.

Lastman was among the main innovators in history painting. He rejected
the high-blown language of his predecessors and believed that a history painting should have the feel of events observed in real life. Lastman took pains to
unite the landscape and the figures; he captured vivid, expressive gestures and
introduced a wealth of carefully rendered details.

His paintings enjoyed great success among his contemporaries. They also
exerted a strong influence on the young Rembrandt, evident not only in the
compositional methods and painterly technique that Rembrandt mastered during his six months in Lastman's studio but also, and more importantly, in the
search for a realistic, expressive approach to history painting that he shared
with his teacher.

PROVENANCE: Acquired by the Hermitage
before 1797; sold in 1854 at an auction of
Hermitage paintings; subsequently in the
Volkov, Korotshevtsov, and Solovev
collections; returned to the Hermitage in
1938 through the State Purchasing
Commission
HERMITAGE CATALOGUES: 1958, II, p. 210;
1981, p. 141
EXHIBITIONS: 1956 Moscow–Leningrad,
p. 80; 1969 Leningrad, no. 54; 1985
Rotterdam, no. 18
LITERATURE: Semenov 1885, I, pp. 158–59;
Semenov 1906a, p. XXXI; Freise 1911, p. 32,
no. 2; Wrangel 1913, p. 91, no. 162;
Shcherbacheva 1940, pp. 40–41, no. 8;
Tümpel 1974, pls. 43, 45; Wittrock 1974,
pp. 10–11; Tümpel 1980, II, p. 145;
Kuznetsov and Linnik 1982, pl. 119

IL

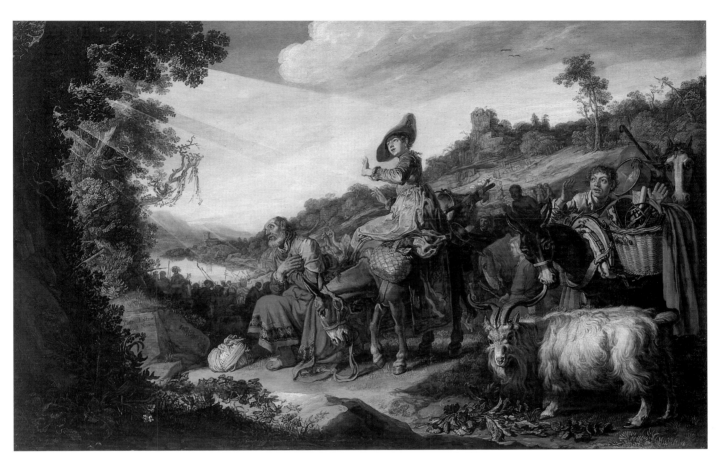

17

GABRIEL METSU

1629 Leiden–1667 Amsterdam

Thought to have studied with Gerard Dou in Leiden. Influenced by Jan Steen and Johannes Vermeer. Worked in Leiden (in 1648 was a founder of the painters' guild) and Amsterdam (1657–67). Painted genre scenes and, more rarely, historical compositions.

18.   *The Doctor's Visit*

Oil on canvas, 24 × 18⅞ in. (61 × 48 cm.)
Signed upper left above door: G Metsu
Inv. no. 919

Among Dutch genre painters Gabriel Metsu is distinguished by his refined and subtle painting and his interest in conveying the emotional state of his protagonists. Though he used the subject matter and pictorial structure of his contemporaries, Metsu sometimes escaped the confines of simply recording everyday life by investing a standard subject with his own more profound and more subtle understanding of life. This is evident in both *The Sick Woman* (Staatliche Museen, Berlin-Dahlem) and the poignant *The Sick Child* (Rijksmuseum, Amsterdam). In the Hermitage's *The Doctor's Visit*, however, the subject is treated with a certain duality. The sinister figure of the doctor, enveloped in his black cloak, the half-swooning young woman, and the room shrouded in semi-darkness all convey the impression of some tragic event. Yet at the same time the symbolic accessories and the slyly inquiring look on the old woman's face are traditional allusions to the possible cause of the young lady's illness—a lover's tryst may perhaps have led to an unexpected pregnancy.

The theme of the doctor visiting a young lady is frequently encountered in Dutch painting and is usually treated in a playfully frivolous manner. The lover's ailment, known in seventeenth-century Holland as *soetepijn*, *minne-pijn*, or *minne koorts*, was hinted at by such details as love letters, statues of cupids, suggestive paintings on the walls, ribbons dipped in urine, which were used to diagnose pregnancy, and so forth. Some of these details are present in the Hermitage painting. The doctor was an indispensable figure in such a situation and, dressed in his semitheatrical attire and flaunting his pseudoscientific knowledge, would have been understood by contemporaries as a comic character in the commedia dell'arte tradition.

Most scholars believe that the picture was painted in the 1660s, arguing that the high quality of the work places it at the very peak of the artist's creative powers. A copy by Pieter van Slingeland is in the Art Gallery and Museum, Glasgow. There is also a drawing treating the subject in a similar manner, formerly in the H. Oppenheimer collection, London, which Regteren Altena (1963) has identified as a copy by Matthijs van den Bergh.

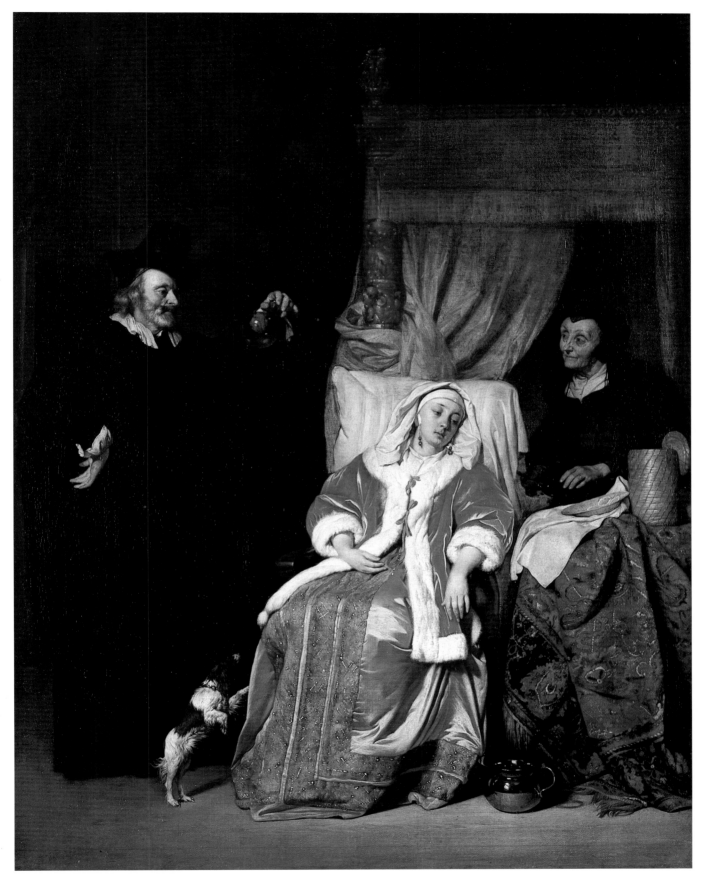

18

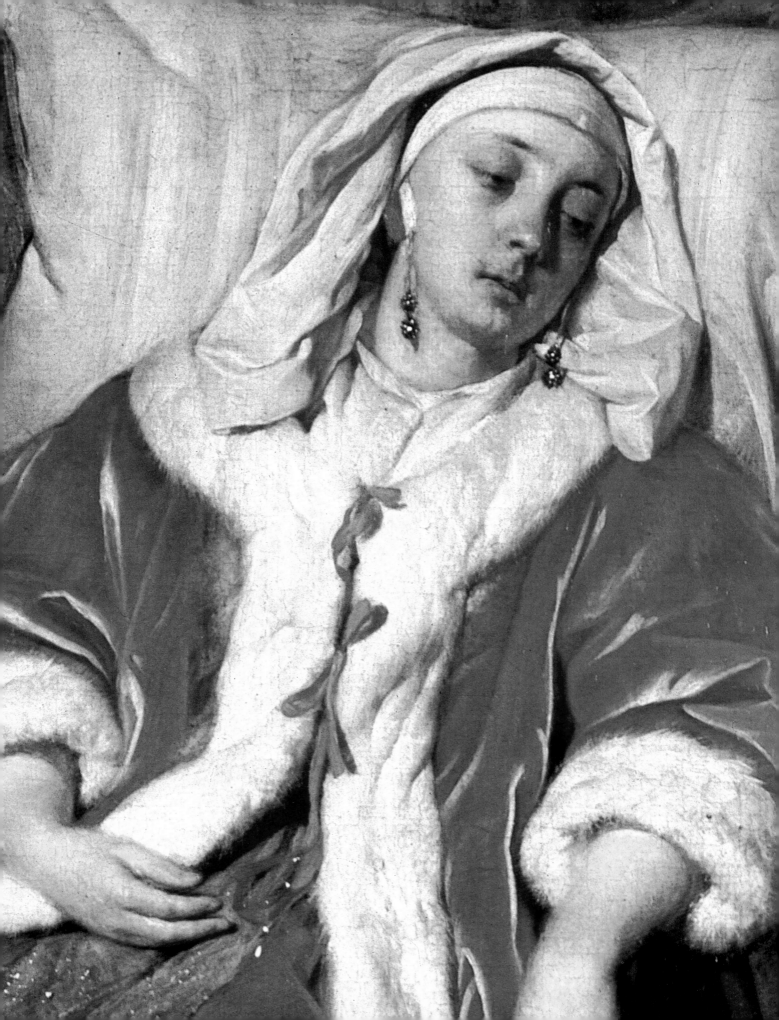

PROVENANCE: Acquired by the Hermitage in 1767 at sale of the Jean de Julienne collection, Paris; until 1702 was in the Jan Agges collection, Amsterdam

HERMITAGE CATALOGUES: 1774, no. 566; 1863–1916, no. 878; 1958, II, p. 218; 1981, p. 147

EXHIBITIONS: 1974 Le Havre, no. 22; 1981 Madrid, p. 44; 1985 Rotterdam, no. 19

LITERATURE: Livret 1838, XXX, no. 26; Waagen 1864, p. 195; Hofstede de Groot 1907, I, no. 114; Pappé 1927, p. 15; Regteren Altena 1963, pp. 13–19; Robinson 1974, pp. 57, 85, note 102; Kuznetsov and Linnik 1982, pl. 107

KS

◁ Detail: Plate 18

ISAACK VAN OSTADE

1621 Haarlem–1649 Haarlem
Studied with his brother Adriaen van Ostade. Worked in Haarlem. Painted
landscapes and scenes from peasant life.

19. *The Frozen Waterway*
    Oil on canvas, 23¼ × 31¾ in. (59 × 80.5 cm.)
    Signed and dated lower right on wall of house: Isaack
        van Ostade 1648
    Inv. no. 907

With his paintings of trees and canals, shown in both summer and winter and
enlivened by many figures, Isaack van Ostade occupies a place midway between
landscape painter and genre painter. He was the younger brother and pupil of
the well-known painter Adriaen van Ostade, and his early works show his
brother's influence. By the mid-1640s, however, Isaack van Ostade had developed
a style of his own, marked by considerable mastery of composition and execution.
The Frozen Waterway is the work of a fully mature painter capable of rendering
aerial perspective and capturing the effect of sunlight breaking through clouds
hovering over water.

Hofstede de Groot mistakenly dated the painting 1642, noting, however,
that the last number was unclear. After a thorough study of the signature and
the date, Kuznetsov (1960) discovered that the final number was not a 2 but an
8 written on its side.

PROVENANCE: Acquired by the Hermitage
in 1769 from the Brühl collection, Dresden
HERMITAGE CATALOGUES: 1774, no. 386;
1863–1916, no. 964; 1958, II, p. 235; 1981,
p. 156
EXHIBITIONS: 1960a Leningrad, no. 43; 1974
Le Havre, no. 16; 1983 Tokyo, no. 13; 1985
Rotterdam, no. 20

LITERATURE: Livret 1838, p. 24, no. 50; Smith
1842, IX, suppl. 10; Waagen 1864, pp. 210–11;
Neustroyev 1898, p. 243; Hofstede de Groot
1910, III, no. 262; Benois [1910], p. 39;
Tartakovskaya 1935, p. 16; Kuznetsov 1960;
Fechner 1963, p. 74, nos. 167, 177

KS

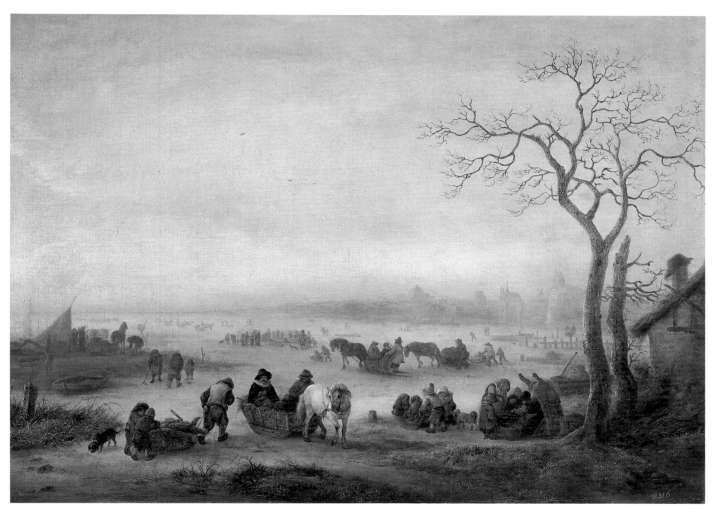

19

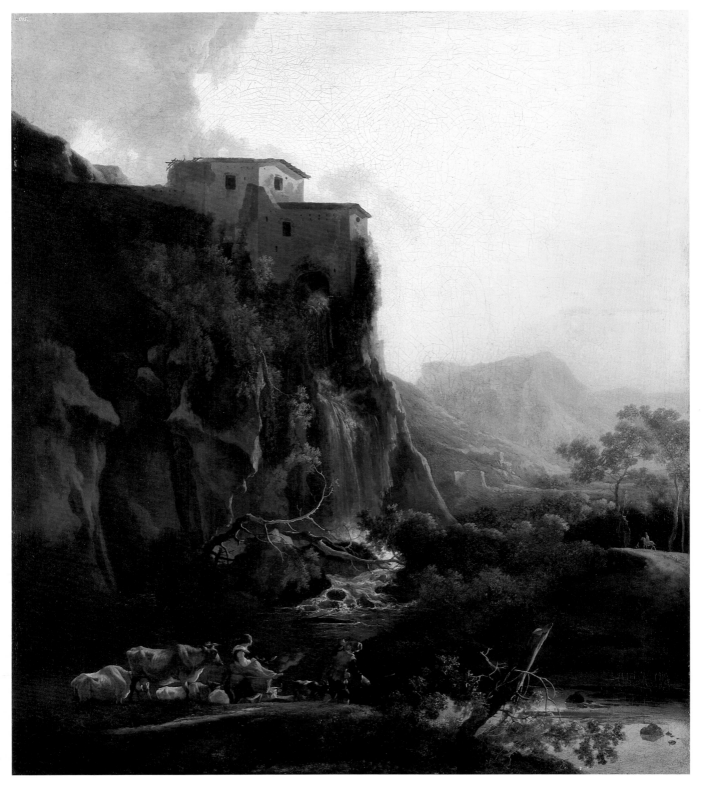

20

ADAM PYNACKER

1621 Pijnakker–1673 Amsterdam
Painter and engraver. Worked in Delft (1649), Schiedam (1657–58), and
Amsterdam. Traveled to Italy. Painted Italianate landscapes.

20. *Mountain Landscape with a Waterfall*
Oil on canvas, 27½ × 23⅝ in. (70 × 60 cm.)
Signed lower right: APynacker (A and P in ligature)
Inv. no. 1096

A waterfall cascading from a tall cliff is the main subject of this elegant landscape with its masterly treatment of sunlight. It is no accident that in the
foreground the artist depicts a shepherd pointing to the cascade of water and
beside him a peasant girl mounted on a donkey. Steland has established that
the waterfall motif was first used as an independent theme about 1640 by
Dutch Italianists working in Rome—Herman van Swanevelt, Jan Both, and
Jan Asselijn (Steland 1984, pp. 85–104). Somewhat later Pynacker also turned
to this theme, and in his earliest work, dated 1654 (Staatliche Museen, Berlin-
Dahlem), he incorporated the waterfall motif. The present painting shows
traces of Jan Both's influence in the slender trees with their fine, translucent
foliage. But hallmarks of the mature Pynacker are already apparent in the
restless outlines of the cliffs, in the broken silhouettes of the bare trunks and
branches, and in the unsettled movements of the staffage group.

PROVENANCE: Acquired by the Hermitage
in 1769 from the Brühl collection, Dresden
HERMITAGE CATALOGUES: 1774, no. 313;
1863–1916, no. 1166; 1958, II, p. 237; 1981,
p. 158
EXHIBITIONS: 1983 Tokyo, no. 17

LITERATURE: Livret 1838, p. 112, no. 15;
Waagen 1864, p. 247; Bode 1873, p. 43;
Shcherbacheva 1924, p. 13; Hofstede de Groot
1926, IX, no. 57; Fechner 1963, p. 121, ills.
90, 91; Steland 1984

IS

PAULUS POTTER

1625 Enkhuizen–1654 Amsterdam
Studied with his father, Pieter Salomonsz Potter, and possibly also with Claes
Moeyaert. Worked in Delft (became a member of the painters' guild in
1646), The Hague (1649–50), and Amsterdam (1652–54). Landscape and
animal painter.

21. *The Watchdog*
Oil on canvas, 38 × 52 in. (96.5 × 132 cm.)
Signed on box at right: Paulus Potter f
Inv. no. 817

Paulus Potter was one of the first Dutch painters to confront the problem of
rendering the effect of daylight on the physical world. His landscapes are
permeated with fresh transparent air and light and with the sense of serene
well-being and tranquillity that distinguishes all mid-seventeenth-century Dutch
painting. Potter's particular interest was animal painting, and he made several
attempts to create a monumental work in this genre. One of the most success-
ful is the present painting. With its dense right section and, on the left, a view
leading off into the distance, the composition recalls Potter's *The Young Bull* of
1647 (Mauritshuis, The Hague). Here Potter has combined his skill as a painter,
his rare powers of observation, his poetic inspiration, and his precision in
recording nature. Describing a similar work by Potter, Eugène Fromentin wrote:
"The animal is its right age, correct in type, in character and temperament, in
length and height, in joint, bone and muscle, in rough and smooth, short and
curly hair, in loose and tight skin—the whole is done to perfection" (Fromentin
1948, p. 120). These words apply equally to the present painting. Six (1907) has
suggested that *The Watchdog* was commissioned by Dirk Tulp, the son of
Potter's patron the physician Nicolaes Tulp, who was earlier Rembrandt's patron. Six believes that Tulp may have brought the dog back with him from
Moscow when he returned from a journey through Russia in 1648.

    The painting's broad brushwork dates it to 1653–54. Hofstede de Groot
(1911, no. 174a) states that a study for the Hermitage painting (oil on wood,
12¼ × 12¼ in. [31.2 × 31.2 cm.]), dated 1653, was sold at the Jan van der
Marck auction, held in Amsterdam, August 25, 1773.

PROVENANCE: Acquired by the Hermitage in 1814 from the collection of Empress Josephine at Malmaison. Previously sold at the Jan van der Marck auction, Amsterdam, in 1773 (no. 248), then at the Naugard collection auction, Paris, in 1780, and subsequently at the auction of the Marquis de Marain collection, Paris (no. 86). The painting was then acquired by the Gemäldegalerie, Kassel, whence it was removed by the French in 1806; bought by Smeet van Alfen and sold at a sale of his paintings in 1810; bought by Lebrun and sold by him in 1811, in Paris; then entered the Malmaison collection

HERMITAGE CATALOGUES: 1863–1916, no. 1055; 1958, II, p. 241; 1981, p. 160
EXHIBITIONS: 1977 Tokyo–Kyoto, no. 20; 1985 Rotterdam, p. 68, no. 21
LITERATURE: Livret 1838, XI, no. 37; Smith 1842, V, no. 34; Waagen 1864, p. 225; Neustroyev 1898, p. 293; Six 1907, VII, pp. 8, 11, 12; Benois [1910], p. 393; Hofstede de Groot 1911, IV, no. 132; Trubnikov 1912, p. 7, no. 9; Tarasov 1983, p. 156

KS

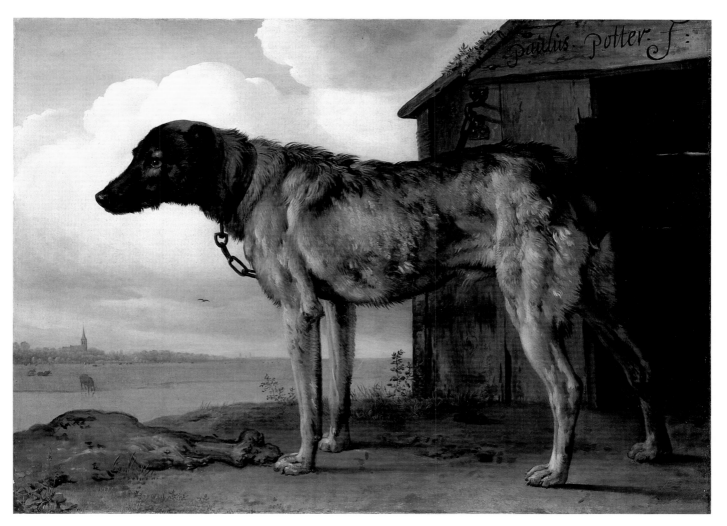

21

REMBRANDT VAN RIJN

1606 Leiden–1669 Amsterdam
Painter, draftsman, and engraver. Pupil of Jacob van Swanenburgh in Leiden
(1624–27) and of Pieter Lastman in Amsterdam (ca. 1631). Had many
pupils, including, in Leiden, Gerard Dou, and, in Amsterdam, Jacob Backer,
Govert Flinck, Gerbrand van den Eeckout, Ferdinand Bol, Philips de
Koninck, Carel Fabritius, Jan Victors, Nicolaes Maes, and Aert de Gelder.
Painted portraits, historical, religious, allegorical, and mythological subjects,
and, more rarely, landscapes.

22. *Flora*
Oil on canvas, 49¼ × 39¾ in. (125 × 101 cm.)
Signed and dated lower left: Rembrandt f. 1634
Inv. no. 732

Here Rembrandt has depicted his first wife, Saskia, as Flora, the Roman goddess of spring and flowers. Saskia was the daughter of Rumbartus van
Uylenburgh, the burgomaster of Leeuwarden. She was betrothed to Rembrandt in 1633, and their marriage took place the following year. Both events
were recorded in Rembrandt's art. Three days after their betrothal he made a
silverpoint drawing of Saskia wearing a broad-brimmed hat decked with flowers
and holding a flower (Kupferstichkabinett, Berlin-Dahlem). The drawing is inscribed in Rembrandt's hand: "This is my wife at the age of twenty-one, three
days after our betrothal, June 8, 1633." Also from that year is a painted portrait
of Saskia (Gemäldegalerie, Dresden). Then in 1634 Rembrandt painted *Flora*,
following it the next year with a second version (National Gallery, London), in
which only the pose of the goddess was substantially altered.

Rembrandt's technique in *Flora* recalls that of his teacher Pieter Lastman,
particularly in the execution of the clothing and the elegant furnishings. But he
has obviously taken great pains to make his brushwork varied and expressive.
In the modeling of the face and hands the strokes flow smoothly into one
another, become thick around the edges and folds of clothing, and are boldly
linear in defining the flowers and foliage.

In the Hermitage's early inventories and catalogues *Flora* was called *The
Young Jewess* and *The Jewish Bride*. These names refer to a 1635 etching by
Rembrandt called *The Great Jewish Bride* (Bartsch 340). There is undoubtedly
a strong similarity between the faces, coiffures, and costumes of the subjects in
the etching and in the London and Leningrad versions of *Flora*. But the title
of the etching, by which it has been known since the eighteenth century, was
purely conventional: in fact it probably depicts the subject of Esther About to
Set Out for Artaxerxes. A preparatory drawing (Benesch 292) in the National-
museum, Stockholm, shows that Saskia was also the model for this etching.

The Hermitage *Flora* appeared at the sale of the Arents collection in
Amsterdam in 1770, under the title *Portrait of a Lady Dressed as a Shepherdess
Shown Full-length Against a Landscape*. In this case the title was not purely
fortuitous, for it was a fashion in Holland in the first half of the seventeenth
century to use costumes of shepherds and shepherdesses in portraits. This
vogue was stimulated by the publication about 1605 of Pieter Cornelisz Hooft's
pastoral romance *Granida and Daifilo*. In 1636 Rembrandt's pupil Govert
Flinck painted companion portraits of his teacher as Daifilo (Rijksmuseum,

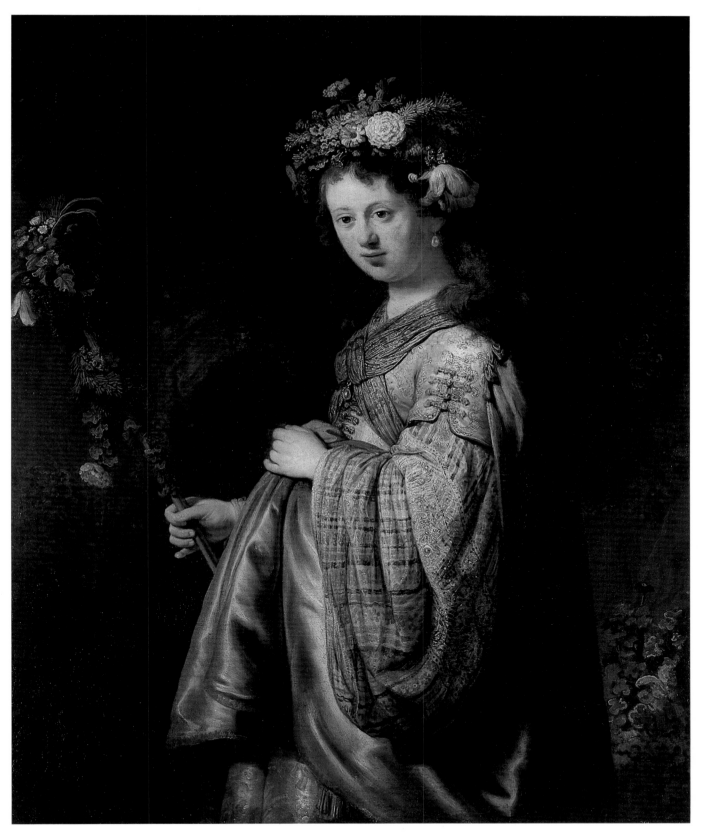

22

Amsterdam) and of Saskia as Granida (Herzog Anton Ulrich-Museum, Brunswick). This image of Saskia the bride in her flower-trimmed straw hat played an important part in Rembrandt's conception of *Flora*. There is, in addition, a drawing that belongs both chronologically and formally between the Berlin drawing and the Leningrad and London paintings. This is the *Young Woman in a Wide-Brimmed Hat Holding a Crook* (Rijksprentenkabinet, Amsterdam), which Slive (1965) believes to be a study for the figure of Flora. While conceding the formal similarity between the drawing and the two paintings, we are more inclined to believe that the young woman is a shepherdess, because of the flask shown at her right side. If so, this would establish a new stage in the history of *Flora*'s conception. Saskia did in fact pose as a shepherdess, and several scholars, among them Kieser (1941–42) and Maclaren (1960), are still of the opinion that in both *Flora*s Rembrandt depicted his wife as an arcadian shepherdess.

It is this author's opinion that, in the process of working on the painting, Rembrandt abandoned his original intention and decided instead to portray Saskia as the goddess Flora. This change of heart probably came about after he had seen Titian's *Flora* (Galleria degli Uffizi, Florence), which was then in the collection of Alphonso Lopez in Amsterdam. Titian's painting made a profound impression on Rembrandt, and it was this model he had in mind when, in 1656, he used Hendrickje Stoffels as the model for his new *Flora* (Metropolitan Museum, New York).

It is in the seventeenth-century sources that we finally discover the true title of the Hermitage painting. In a note written in 1635 in Rembrandt's own hand on the back of a drawing (Kupferstichkabinett, Berlin-Dahlem; Benesch 448) the artist records the sale of several paintings by his pupils that depict Flora. The assumption that these paintings were copies of the Leningrad and London canvases by Rembrandt is thus proved to be correct, and Michel's theory (1893) can now be confirmed by documentary evidence. As a typical work of the 1630s, permeated with classical mythology, *Flora* fits perfectly into that body of Rembrandt's work inspired by Saskia: *Bellona* (1633; Metropolitan Museum, New York), *Minerva* (1635; J. Weitzner collection, London), and *Sophonisba* (1634; Prado, Madrid). There is an early, partial copy (cut down?; oil on canvas, oval format, 27½ × 21⅝ in. [70 × 55 cm.]) in a private collection in The Hague.

PROVENANCE: Acquired by the Hermitage before 1775; appeared in 1770 at the Harmen Arents auction in Amsterdam
HERMITAGE CATALOGUES: 1863–1916, no. 812; 1958, II, p. 251; 1981, p. 164
EXHIBITIONS: 1956 Moscow–Leningrad, no. 8; 1956 Amsterdam–Rotterdam, no. 24; 1968 Tokyo–Kyoto, no. 3; 1975–76 Washington, D.C., no. 18; 1981 Madrid, p. 481; 1982 Tokyo, no. 3; 1984 Warsaw, no. 1; 1985 Rotterdam, no. 22
LITERATURE: Bode 1883, p. 424; Michel 1893; Voss 1905, p. 158; Valentiner 1909, p. 137; Hofstede de Groot 1915, VI, no. 206; Drost 1926, p. 153; Weisbach 1926, p. 235; Benesch 1935, p. 17; Kieser 1941–42, p. 155; Hamann 1948, pp. 215, 216; Rosenberg 1948, I, p. 43; Levinson-Lessing 1956, p. 8; Maclaren 1960, pp. 333–34; Held 1961, pp. 201–18; Slive 1965, II, no. 312; Gerson 1968, no. 92; Haak 1968, p. 104; Levinson-Lessing 1971, no. 7; Rembrandt 1971, no. 9; Louttit 1973, pp. 317–26; Kettering 1983, pp. 19–44; Rembrandt Corpus 1982–86, no. 93; Tümpel 1986, pp. 110, 115, no. 104

IL

Detail: Plate 22 ▷

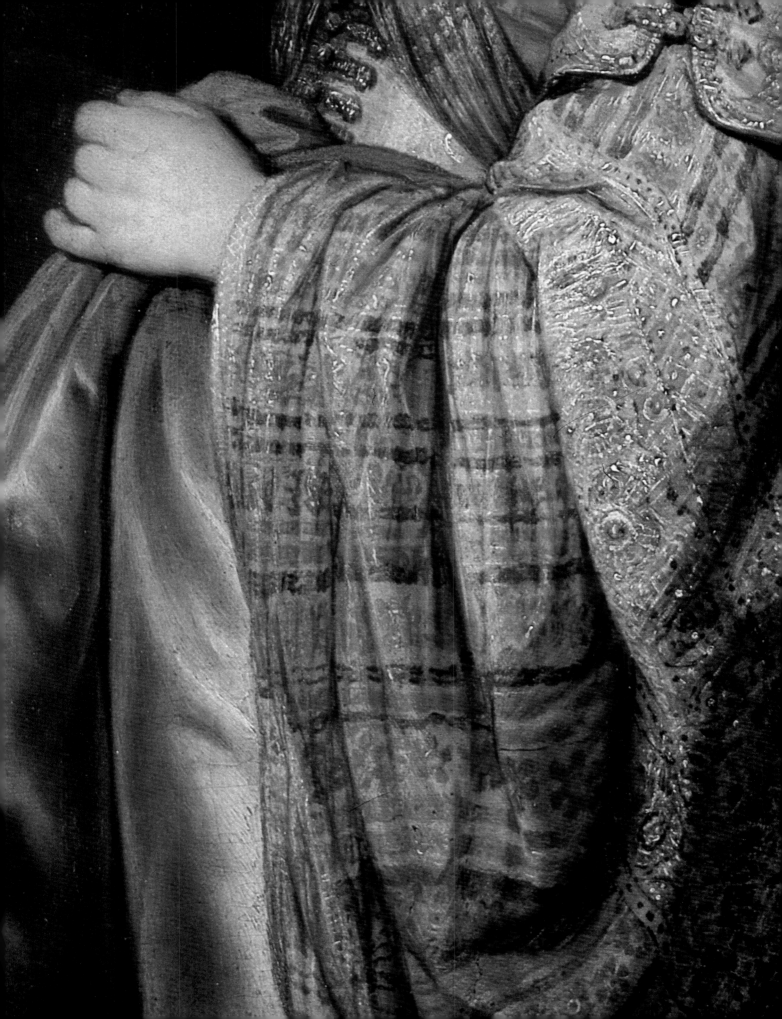

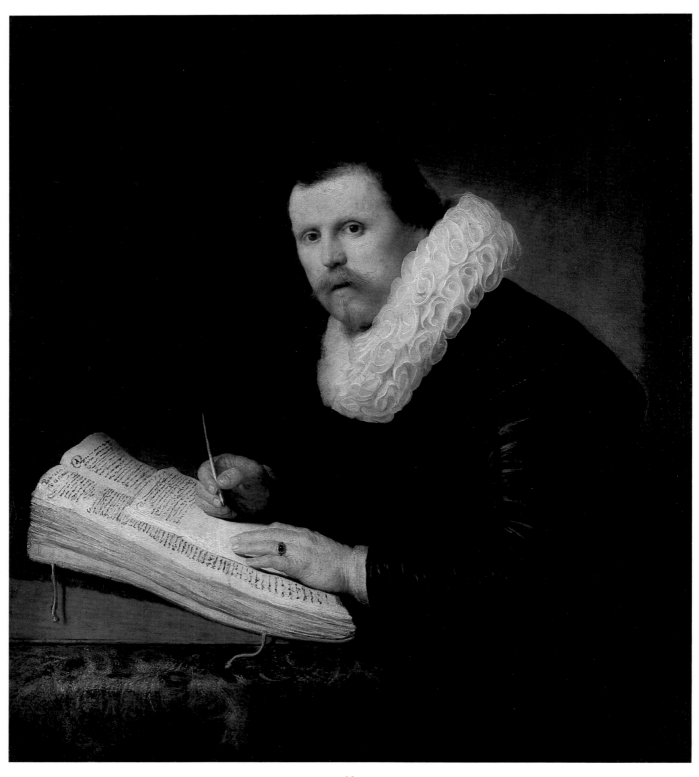

23

REMBRANDT VAN RIJN

23. *Portrait of a Scholar*
Oil on canvas, 41 × 36¼ in. (104 × 92 cm.)
Signed and dated lower right: RHL 1631
Inv. no. 744

Early in autumn 1631 Rembrandt moved from Leiden to Amsterdam. Houbraken (1718) remarked, "In order to paint portraits and other pictures he often had occasion to be in Amsterdam, and seeing that conditions in this city were favorable and might lead to his advancement, he considered it useful to make it his permanent place of residence."

The portraits that occasioned Rembrandt's frequent trips to Amsterdam in 1631, and his subsequent move there, still survive. These are the portrait of the Amsterdam merchant Nicolaes Ruts (Frick Collection, New York) and the Hermitage's so-called *Portrait of a Scholar.* At one time, on the basis of a conjecture by Waagen (1864), the portrait was thought to be of the famous Amsterdam calligrapher Lieven Coppenol. Later, when comparison with an authentic portrait of Coppenol ruled out Waagen's suggestion, scholars were divided in their opinions. Bode (1883) surmised that the sitter was a professor at Leiden University; Hamann (1948) and Bredius (1969) suggested that he was an Amsterdam or Leiden scholar. It is possible, however, that the sitter was not a scholar but rather a public servant or a municipal employee.

Rembrandt followed contemporary Flemish models in painting his first large commissioned portraits, and the *Portrait of a Scholar* was modeled on Rubens's *Caspar Gevartius* (Royal Museum of Fine Arts, Antwerp), of about 1628. In reworking the prototype, however, he nearly eliminated the posed quality that Rubens emphasized. The sense of stiff formality disappears, and the portrait becomes simpler and more intimate. In his effort to make the painting lifelike Rembrandt has captured the sitter with his hands paused in the act of writing. The slight edge of irritation in the scholar's expression is psychologically convincing in a man interrupted at his work. The painting's limited palette —the blacks and whites of the clothing and the gray-green background—the smooth contours around the light and dark patches, and the unusual, almost square format all convey an aura of seriousness, solidity, and stability.

The artist's brushwork is likewise calm and measured. It follows each shape closely, revealing its volume and texture. The viewer not only sees but as it were feels the soft skin of the hands, the cool page of the open book, the loose weave of the tablecloth. These objects provide contrasts in color and in texture, with the artist emphasizing their essential differences.

PROVENANCE: Acquired by the Hermitage in 1769 from the Brühl collection, Dresden
HERMITAGE CATALOGUES: 1863–1916, no. 808; 1958, II, p. 251; 1981, p. 164
EXHIBITIONS: 1936 Moscow–Leningrad, no. 3; 1938 Leningrad, no. 144; 1956 Moscow–Leningrad, pp. 40–50; 1968 Tokyo–Kyoto, no. 1; 1968–69 Belgrade, no. 35; 1969 Leningrad, no. 2; 1982 Tokyo, no. 1
LITERATURE: Waagen 1864; Bode 1883, 1864; Valentiner 1909, p. 65; Hofstede de Groot 1915, VI, no. 775; Weislach 1926, p. 265; Benesch 1935, p. 11; Hamann 1948, p. 138; Knattel 1956, p. 45; Levinson-Lessing 1956, p. VI; Bauch 1966, no. 349; Gersch 1968, no. 54; Bredius 1969, no. 146; Levinson-Lessing 1971, no. 3; Rembrandt Corpus 1986, II, A44; Tümpel 1986, p. 77, no. 191

IL

REMBRANDT VAN RIJN

24. The Sacrifice of Isaac

Oil on canvas (transferred to a new canvas), 76 × 52¼ in.
   (193 × 132.5 cm.)
Signed and dated lower left: Rembrandt. f. 1635
Inv. no. 727

During the mid-1630s Rembrandt's art coincided most closely with the prevailing Baroque style. The large painting *The Sacrifice of Isaac* dates from this period. Rembrandt has chosen to depict the most dramatic moment of the Old Testament narrative (Gen. 22:10–12): the father's dagger is about to pierce the son's throat when an angel appears and stops the sacrifice. The suddenness of these events is underscored by the dagger falling from Abraham's hand and the expression of terrified amazement on his face. The composition has been conceived as a beautiful and elegant theatrical spectacle. The fluttering folds of Abraham's cloak and his disheveled hair; the restless flashes of light falling on Isaac's face, hands, and naked body; and the jagged outlines and dynamic splashes of color create an effect of heightened drama. Held (1969) noted the painting's theatrical composition and suggested that Rembrandt may have been familiar with *Abraham Making His Sacrifice*, a play by Theodore Beza (1519–1605) that emphasized the aspects of Abraham's behavior and emotional state that are highlighted in the painting.

The following year Rembrandt returned to this theme in a drawing (British Museum, London; Benesch 90), after which one of his pupils executed a painting in 1636 (Alte Pinakothek, Munich). The main compositional innovations in this version are the altered pose of the angel and the addition of a lamb caught in the bushes, which is to take Isaac's place on the sacrificial pyre. The Munich painting owes a great deal to a picture by Pieter Lastman on the same subject. (Lastman's painting exists in two versions: one, dated 1616, is in the Louvre; the other has not survived and is known only through an engraving by J. van Somer.) The angel is shown flying toward Abraham, not from the left as in the Hermitage painting, but from behind, as in Lastman's. Weisbach (1926) has shown that the angel in the Hermitage canvas has its prototype in Titian's *Sacrifice*, painted for the ceiling of the Church of Santa Maria della Salute, Venice. But both the Hermitage and Munich paintings retain the expressive gesture of Lastman's angel.

The Hermitage painting was engraved in 1781 by John Murphy and published in Walpole's *Set of Prints . . .* , 1788, no. XXIII (Le Blanc 1854–59, III, p. 73, Murphy no. 1).

PROVENANCE: Acquired by the Hermitage in 1779 from the Walpole collection, Houghton Hall, England (acquired by Walpole in 1767); previously sold in Amsterdam, September 16, 1760 (no. 1).
HERMITAGE CATALOGUES: 1863–1916, no. 792; 1958, II, p. 252; 1981, p. 164
EXHIBITIONS: 1936 Moscow–Leningrad, no. 8; 1956 Moscow–Leningrad, p. 51; 1968 Tokyo–Kyoto, no. 5; 1969 Amsterdam, no. 4a; 1969 Leningrad, no. 8; 1982 Tokyo, no. 4
LITERATURE: Bode 1883, p. 431; Valentiner 1909, p. 170; Hofstede de Groot 1915, VI, no. 9; Bandissin 1925, pp. 152–54; Weisbach 1926, pp. 63, 188; Müller 1929, pp. 64–67; Benesch 1935, p. 18; Hamann 1948, pp. 249, 259–61; Rosenberg 1948, pp. 105, 225; Knuttel 1956, p. 93; Levinson-Lessing 1956, p. VIII; Moltke 1965, p. 13; Brochagen and Knuttel 1967, pp. 72–75; Gerson 1968, no. 74; Haak 1968, p. 126; Bredius 1969, no. 498; Held 1969, pp. 122–24, no. 29; Stechow 1969, p. 150; Bruyn 1970, p. 39, no. 1; Levinson-Lessing 1971, no. 10; Tümpel 1986, p. 164, no. 9

IL

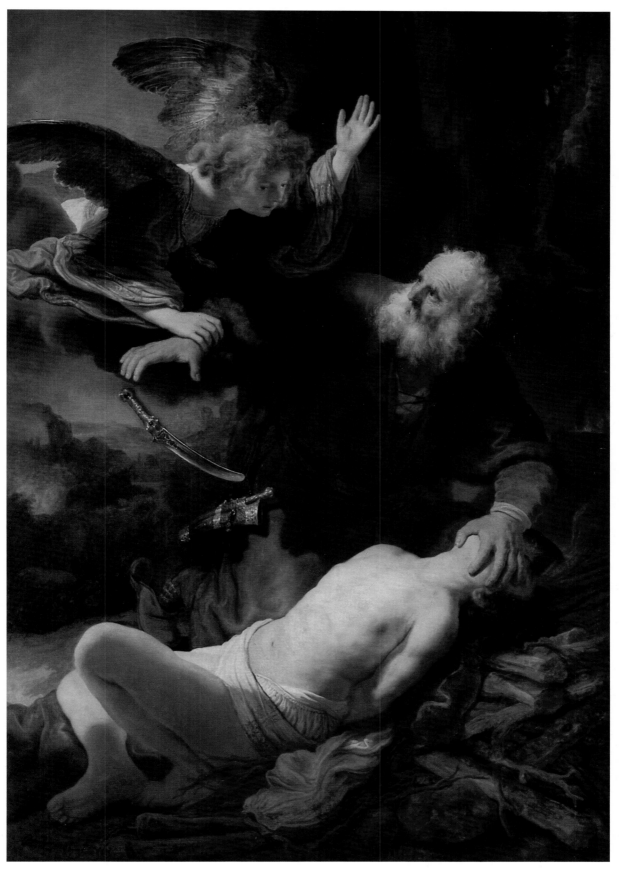

24

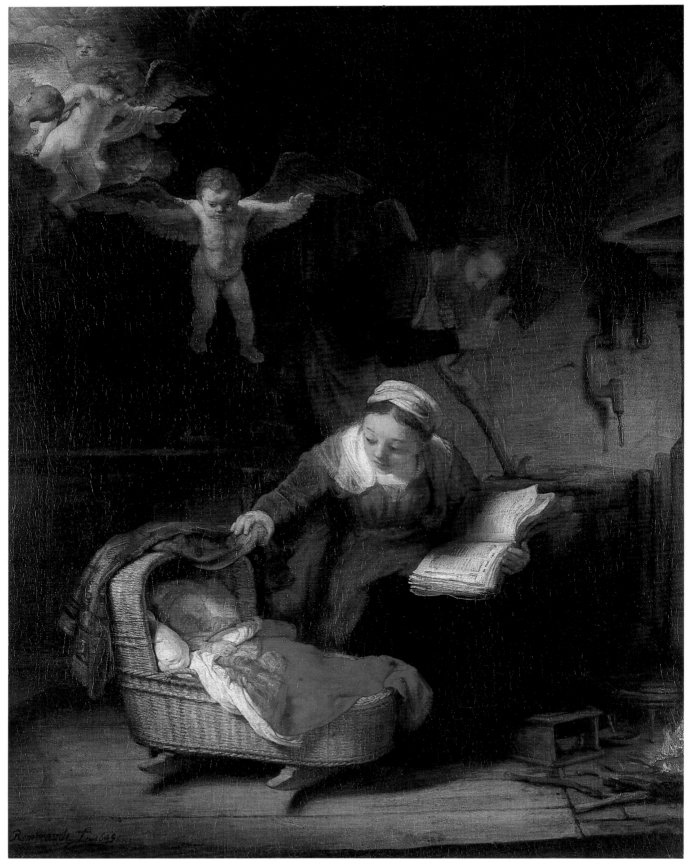

REMBRANDT VAN RIJN

25. *The Holy Family*

Oil on canvas, 46⅛ × 35⅞ in. (117 × 91 cm.). A strip of canvas
1 in. (2.5 cm.) wide has been added at the top, and a concealed
strip ⅝ in. (1.5 cm.) wide has been added at the bottom
Signed and dated bottom left: Rembrandt f. 1645
Inv. no. 741

In the 1640s Rembrandt painted a series of canvases depicting the Holy Family, the finest of which is the present work. Rembrandt's treatment so much resembles a genre scene that the painting might well be called *The Carpenter's Family*. Rembrandt's *Holy Family* is not, however, merely a scene from everyday life, found so often in Dutch art, but a work suffused with a profound lyricism. The painting is based on preparatory studies, and the figure of Mary may well have been modeled directly on Hendrickje Stoffels, the young peasant girl who entered Rembrandt's house as a servant and became his devoted companion. Three drawings have survived which are undoubtedly related to the painting. One of these is a general compositional sketch showing the Holy Family seated (L. Clark collection, Cambridge, Mass.; Benesch 569) and possibly depicting Joseph's Dream, the event preceding the Flight into Egypt. According to the New Testament, however, this episode should show a single angel rather than little cherubs, warning Joseph that Jesus is in danger, and it is this scene that Rembrandt depicts in another painting, of 1645, in the Staatliche Museen, Berlin-Dahlem (Bredius 569). In the Clark drawing the group of cherubs and the basket in which the Infant Jesus lies are shown in great detail and are very close to the painting. The second drawing directly related to the Hermitage picture is a general sketch in the Musée Bonnat, Bayonne (Bredius 567). Finally, the H. Oppenheimer collection contained a sketch of the basket with the sleeping infant which is an exact replica of the motif in the Hermitage work. The *Sketch of the Head of a Seated Girl* (private collection, United States; Bredius 375), which is also considered a study for this painting, now appears to be a partial copy by Rembrandt's pupils, as suggested by Gerson (1968).

PROVENANCE: Acquired by the Hermitage in 1772 from the Crozat collection, Paris; before 1740 in the Pierre Crozat collection, Paris; before 1750 in the collection of François Crozat, baron du Chatelle, Paris; before 1772 in the Crozat collection of Baron de Thiers, Paris; appeared at the Adraien Bouth sale, The Hague, 1733
HERMITAGE CATALOGUES: 1883–1916, no. 796; 1958, II, p. 256; 1981, p. 165
EXHIBITIONS: 1936 Moscow–Leningrad, no. 16; 1956 Amsterdam–Rotterdam, no. 50; 1969 Leningrad, no. 15; 1981 Madrid, pp. 41–48; 1982 Tokyo, no. 5; 1985 Rotterdam, no. 23
LITERATURE: Bode 1883, p. 476; Valentiner 1909, p. 281; Hofstede de Groot 1915, VI, no. 94; Weisbach 1926, pp. 154, 156; Benesch 1935, pp. 36–37; Hamann 1948, pp. 287, 289; Rosenberg 1948, pp. 51, 121–22; Levinson-Lessing 1956, p. 11; Bauch 1966, no. 73; Gerson 1968, no. 211; Haak 1968, pp. 188–89; Bredius 1969, no. 570; Levinson-Lessing 1971, no. 16; Tümpel 1986, pp. 245–46, no. 65

IL

REMBRANDT VAN RIJN

26. *Haman Recognizes His Fate (David and Uriah?)*
Oil on canvas (doubled), 50 × 45⅝ in. (127 × 116 cm.)
Signed lower right: Rembrandt
Inv. no. 752

In his late historical paintings Rembrandt avoided detailed storytelling. As a consequence there are a number of paintings whose subject matter is extremely difficult to decipher and which remain somewhat enigmatic. The Hermitage's *Haman Recognizes His Fate* is one such work.

For many decades following its acquisition in 1769 the painting was known as *Haman's Disgrace* because it was thought to illustrate the events narrated in Esther 4–6. Despite the fact that neither the characters (with the exception of the principal figure) nor their psychological state correspond to the biblical narrative, the traditional attribution remained unchallenged until the twentieth century. Valentiner (1921) suggested that the canvas depicted an event from 2 Samuel 11:1–27. This theory was supported by Linnik (1956), and the painting was given the title *David and Uriah*. Valentiner suggested yet another reading of the subject in 1957: *Jonathan Leaves Saul's Feast* (1 Kings 20:24–34). But here too the mood of the protagonist had little in common with the biblical story.

As early as 1911 Hofstede de Groot, in his book *Rembrandt's Bible*, had interpreted the painting's traditional title as a reference to events described in Esther 7 rather than 6. Ahbel (1964–65) and Kahr (1965) arrived at the same conclusion, as did Tümpel (1968). Nevertheless, this reading also failed to account fully for the content of the painting, and Nieuwstraten (1967) rejected it, arguing instead that the painting had been cut down and had thus lost details essential for a correct reading of the story. However, examination of the edges of the canvas negates the hypothesis that the canvas was substantially cut down and once contained major figures or details that might have shed some light on the subject.

The powerful psychological insight with which the central figure is painted makes this one of Rembrandt's most impressive works. The gray, pinched face beneath an enormous turban seems small and pathetic against the luxurious crimson clothing, a color-saturated combination of red and ocher brushwork. By contrast the figures in the background are painted in a different palette and a less intense, rather simplified psychological key. It is as if, having put all his strength and emotion into his protagonist, Rembrandt saw these secondary figures only as an accompaniment to the sufferings of the hero. This impression of disparity is strengthened by the scale of the figures: those in the background are reduced more drastically than the distance separating them from the foreground demands. In fact several specialists have questioned whether the background figures are by Rembrandt himself.

The painting is generally dated to about 1665.

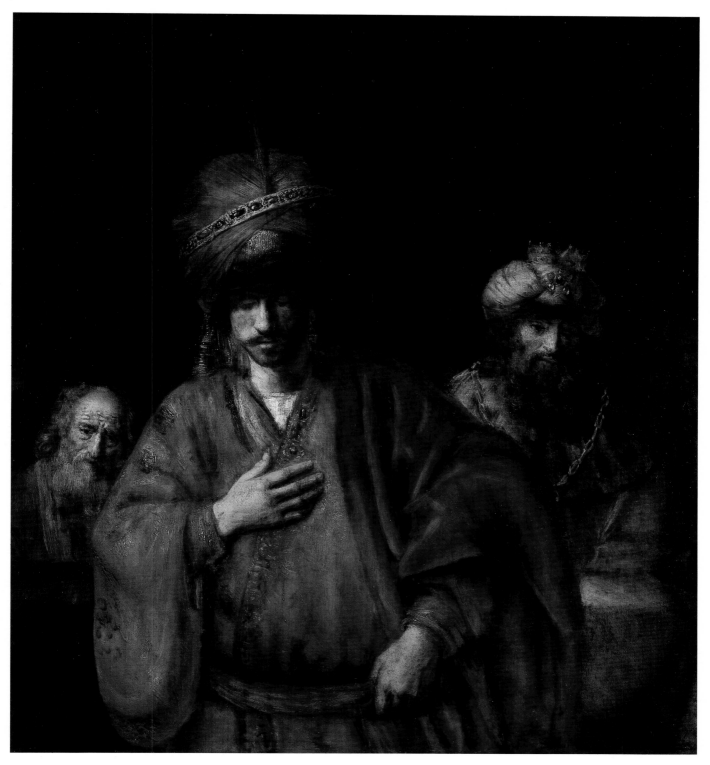

26

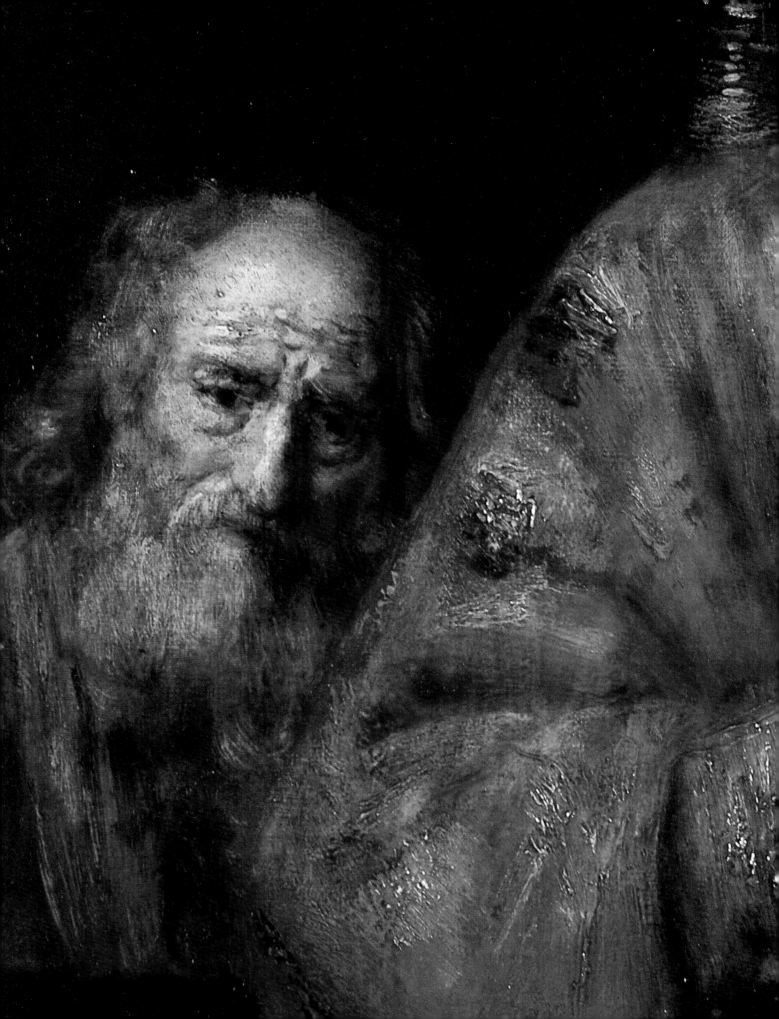

PROVENANCE: Acquired by the Hermitage in 1769 from the John Blackwood collection, London. Previously sold at the Six collection auction, Amsterdam, May 13, 1734
HERMITAGE CATALOGUES: 1863–1916, no. 795; 1958, II, p. 259; 1981, p. 165
EXHIBITIONS: 1936 Moscow–Leningrad, no. 27; 1956 Moscow–Leningrad, no. 61; 1969 Leningrad, no. 23; 1975–76 Washington, D.C., no. 19; 1981 Vienna, pp. 100–103; 1982 Tokyo, no. 10
LITERATURE: Bode 1883, p. 479; Valentiner 1909, p. 469; Hofstede de Groot 1915, VI, no. 48; Valentiner 1921, p. 128; Weisbach 1926, pp. 476, 594; Hamann 1948, pp. 412, 413; Knuttel 1956, p. 208; Levinson-Lessing 1956, p. XIX; Linnik 1956, pp. 46–50; Bialostocki 1957, p. 210; Linnik 1957, pp. 8–12; Valentiner 1957, pp. 229–30; Levinson-Lessing 1964, no. 84; Ahbel 1964–65; Kahr 1965, pp. 258–73; Bauch 1966, no. 39; Nieuwstraten 1967, pp. 61–63; Gerson 1968, no. 357; Kahr 1968, pp. 63–68; Tümpel 1968, pp. 106–12; Bredius 1969, no. 531; Levinson-Lessing 1971, no. 29; Tümpel 1986, pp. 315–16, no. 31

IL

◁ Detail: Plate 26

REMBRANDT VAN RIJN

27. *Portrait of an Old Jew*

Oil on canvas (relined), 42⅞ × 33⅜ in. (109 × 84.8 cm.),
   including strips added to the bottom and sides; 35 × 30⅛ in.
   (89 × 76.5 cm.) minus the strips
Signed and dated in left background near the shoulder:
   Rembrandt f. 1654
Inv. no. 737

The United Provinces were known for their great religious tolerance and gave
refuge to Jews fleeing the Inquisition in Italy and Portugal. The majority of
them lived in Amsterdam on the Jodenbreestraat, where Rembrandt's house
was situated. As a devoted reader and interpreter of the Bible, Rembrandt
found in this milieu the models for his biblical and evangelical compositions;
he also made etchings and paintings of his Jewish friends, many of whose
names are unknown. One of these anonymous sitters was the old man with the
wise and expressive face who posed for the present portrait. His unconven-
tional clothing suggests that this was no standard commissioned portrait. The
expressiveness of the image has been created by what seem to be extremely
limited means: the figure posed symmetrically in the form of a broad-based
triangle, the folds of the clothing falling freely and rhythmically. This compositional austerity adds to the portrait's monumental grandeur, while the sitter
himself conveys great spiritual strength.

   This portrait may be a companion piece to the *Portrait of an Old Woman*,
also in the Hermitage (inv. no. 738), although there are as yet no grounds to
conclude that the two models were a married couple.

   Tümpel (1986) maintains firmly that the two paintings are not portraits
but are depictions of historical personages who appear in the narrative paintings of Rembrandt and his pupils.

PROVENANCE: Acquired by the Hermitage
in 1781 from the Baudouin collection, Paris
HERMITAGE CATALOGUES: 1863–1916, no. 810;
1958, p. 259; 1981, p. 165
EXHIBITIONS: 1936 Moscow–Leningrad, no.
22; 1938 Leningrad, no. 148; 1956 Moscow–
Leningrad, p. 57; 1968 Tokyo–Kyoto,
no. 8; 1972 Leningrad, no. 377; 1979–80
Melbourne–Sydney, no. 24; 1981 Madrid,
no. 9; 1982 Tokyo, no. 6; 1984 Warsaw, no. 2

LITERATURE: Bode 1873, p. 810; Bode 1883,
p. 503; Valentiner 1909, p. 427; Hofstede
de Groot 1915, VI, no. 439; Weisbach 1926,
p. 550; Benesch 1935, p. 54; Hamann 1948,
p. 392; Rosenberg 1948, p. 59; Levinson-
Lessing 1958, p. 259; Egorova 1966, pp.
85–86; Bauch 1966, no. 210; Gerson 1968,
no. 313; Bredius 1969, no. 270; Levinson-
Lessing 1971, no. 20; Tümpel 1986, p. 302,
no. 141

IL

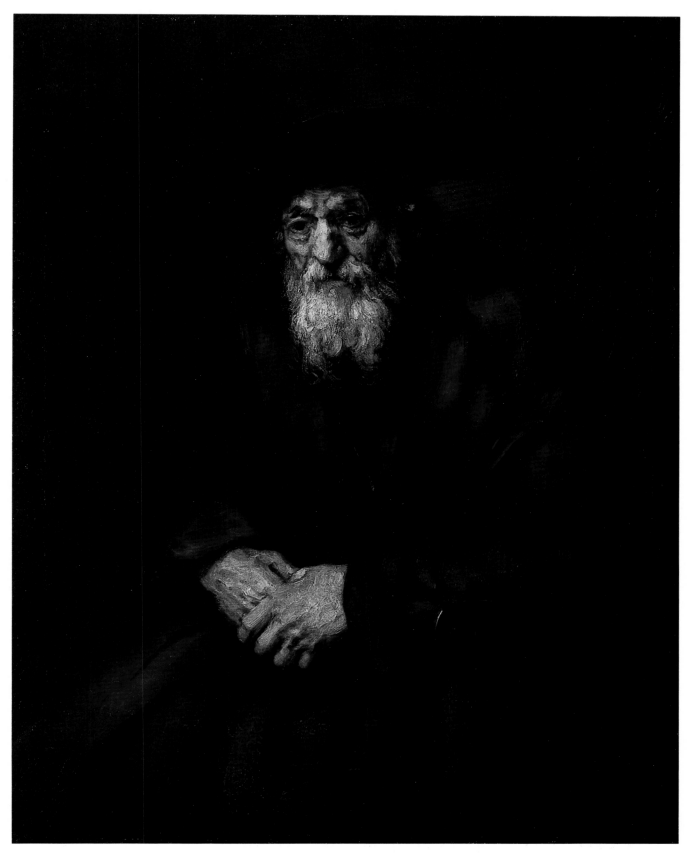

27

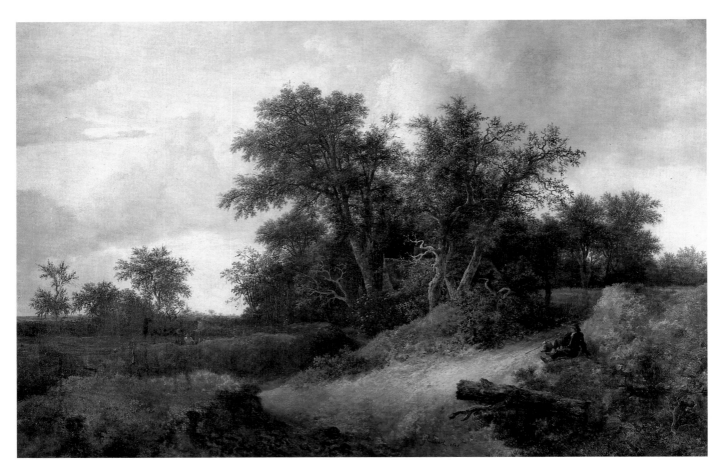

28

JACOB VAN RUISDAEL

1628/29 Haarlem–1682 Amsterdam
A nephew and possibly a pupil of Salomon van Ruysdael, whose influence
can be seen in van Ruisdael's early works. Also influenced by Cornelis
Vroom. Traveled in Germany with the painter Nicolaes Berchem (ca. 1650).
Worked in Haarlem (a member of the painters' guild from 1648) and later in
Amsterdam (from 1657).

28. *Small House in a Grove*
Oil on canvas, 41¼ × 64¼ in. (105 × 163 cm.)
Signed and dated right center: JvRuisdael 1646
   (J, v, and R in ligature)
Inv. no. 939

Small House in a Grove is one of the earliest dated works by Jacob van Ruisdael.
Two years after he painted it, in 1648, the young artist was admitted to the
Haarlem Guild of Saint Luke. His mature handling of the duny landscape, his
careful observation of and his precision in depicting plant motifs, and his
ability to focus on essentials are evidence of his exceptional individuality as an
artist. As Hofstede de Groot (1911) noted, "it is hard to believe that this is the
work of a seventeen-year-old youth."

The subject of the painting, the choice of motifs, and the color scheme
indicate the painters who influenced van Ruisdael in his first years as an independent artist, Cornelis Vroom among them. Similar compositions can be
found in the work of such artists of the older generation as Salomon van
Ruysdael and Jan van Goyen. What is striking in the present painting, however, is the artist's attempt to create a monumental image of nature. This is
particularly evident in the large size of the canvas, so unexpected in the work
of an inexperienced painter.

The composition is dominated by a group of tall trees on a hill, a motif
that reappears in more dramatic form in an etching by van Ruisdael of 1649
(Hollstein 1978, XX, p. 175, no. 6).

There have been several opinions expressed on the staffage in the Hermitage
painting. Hofstede de Groot (1911) maintained that the figures were the work
of another artist. Simon (1930 and 1935) attributed them to Jacob's father,
Isaack van Ruisdael, but as Slive and Hoetink (1981) have correctly noted, this
suggestion seems improbable. Jacob van Ruisdael himself frequently painted
the people and animals in his early works.

A smaller version of this painting (oil on canvas, 27⅛ × 34½ in. [68.8 ×
87.5 cm.]) is in Gouverneurs Huis, Paramaribo, Surinam.

PROVENANCE: Acquired by the Hermitage
before 1838
HERMITAGE CATALOGUES: 1863–1916, no.
1143; 1958, p. 246; 1981, p. 162
EXHIBITIONS: 1981–82 The Hague–
Cambridge, Mass., no. 3
LITERATURE: Waagen 1864, p. 243; Bode
1873, p. 38; Benois [1910], p. 410; Wurzbach

1910, II, p. 520; Hofstede de Groot 1911,
IV, no. 895; Shcherbacheva 1924, p. 21;
Pappé 1926, p. 200; Rosenberg 1928, no.
552; Simon 1930, p. 189 (staffage by Isaack
van Ruisdael); Simon 1935, p. 17 (staffage
by Isaack van Ruisdael); Fechner 1958,
p. 9; Fechner 1963, p. 93, ills. 62, 63; Slive
and Hoetink 1981, no. 3

IS

JACOB VAN RUISDAEL

29. *The Marsh*

Oil on canvas, 28⅝ × 39 in. (72.5 × 99 cm.)
Partially effaced signature lower left: IvRuisdael
    (I, v, and R in ligature)
Inv. no. 934

The Marsh, one of the most renowned paintings in the Hermitage collection, is a key work from Jacob van Ruisdael's finest period. His search for a heroic image of nature finds here its classic fulfillment. Van Ruisdael uses gigantic trees of various ages, grouped in a dense circle around a forest pond, to express the primordial power of nature and to present the eternal cycle of birth, maturity, and decay. For all its external tranquillity this secluded landscape has great tragic power. The thick crowns and convulsively twisted branches of the trees spread out like a tent above the stagnant water, while the solitary figure of a man half-obscured among the powerful trunks is dwarfed by the massive forms. In the 1660s van Ruisdael painted several canvases of similar composition and subject, only one of which he dated (1660; formerly in the H. A. Clowes collection, Norbury, Ashbourne, Derbyshire).

It has long been recognized that the prototype for the present painting was *Stag Hunt in a Marsh* by Roelant Savery (1576–1639). A well-known engraving of *The Marsh* was done by Egidius Sadeler (1570–1629) (Hollstein 1980, XXI, no. 233). Rubens's study *Hunters at Sunrise* (Bayerisches Staatsgemäldesammlungen, Munich) also goes back to Savery's composition, with its theme of the chase and its striking use of the bright distance peeping through the interwoven trunks and branches. Van Ruisdael, however, excludes both of these elements, and in contrast to Savery's fanciful, Mannerist landscape his painting is characterized by clarity and sobriety. Waagen (1864) dates the Hermitage painting to between 1660 and 1670, Rosenberg (1928) to between 1665 and 1669.

PROVENANCE: Acquired by the Hermitage between 1763 and 1774
HERMITAGE CATALOGUES: 1774, no. 1367; 1863–1916, no. 1136; 1958, II, p. 250; 1981, p. 163
EXHIBITIONS: 1975–76 Washington, D.C., no. 3; 1981 Vienna, pp. 118–19; 1981–82 The Hague–Cambridge, Mass., no. 36; 1983 Tokyo, no. 21; 1985 Rotterdam, no. 25
LITERATURE: Smith 1835, VI, no. 306; Livret 1838, no. 4; Somov 1859, p. 114; Waagen 1864, p. 243; Bode 1873, p. 39; Michel 1890, p. 60; Benois [1910], p. 411; Wurzbach 1910, II, p. 520; Hofstede de Groot 1911, IV, no. 508; Roh 1921, p. 331; Shcherbacheva 1924, p. 21; Rosenberg 1928, pp. 48, 49, 91, no. 313, ill. 103; Simon 1930, p. 46; Gerson 1934, p. 79; Bode 1956, p. 232; Fechner 1958, p. 17; Vipper 1962, p. 87; Fechner 1963, pp. 70, 93–94, ills. 66, 68; Stechow 1966, p. 75; Rosenberg, Slive, and Kuile 1972, p. 268, pl. 214; Kuznetsov 1973, XIV, p. 31; Slive and Hoetink 1981, p. 108; Tarasov 1983, p. 221

IS

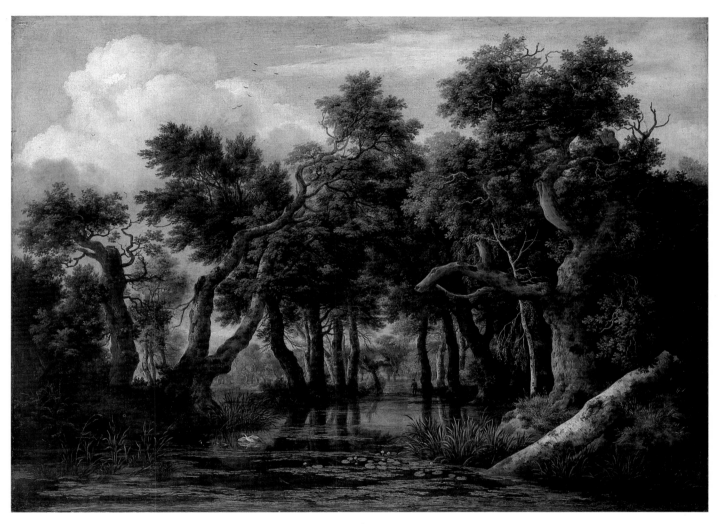

29

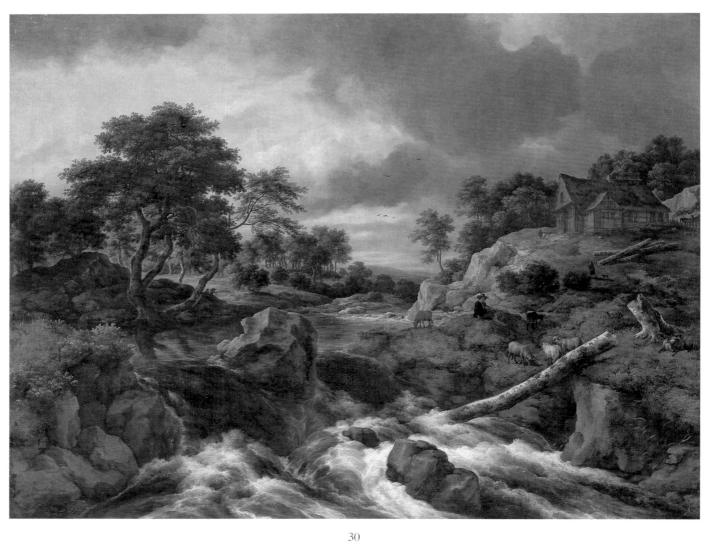

30

JACOB VAN RUISDAEL

30. *Waterfall in Norway*
Oil on canvas, 42½ × 56⅛ in. (108 × 142.5 cm.)
Signed lower right: IvRuisdael (I, v, and R in ligature)
Inv. no. 942

Jacob van Ruisdael first turned to the theme of Scandinavian landscapes in the mid-1660s in a series of vertical paintings. The prospect of grandiose cascades of water, full of power and energy, could not fail to attract an artist whose inspiration fed on heroic images. His northern landscapes are based not on actual observations, however, but on the paintings of his older contemporary Allart van Everdingen (1621–1675), who popularized the treatment of Scandinavian waterfalls in Dutch art. In fact, van Ruisdael never traveled farther than the border region between Holland and Germany, which makes his masterly renderings of the dramatic grandeur of the northern landscape all the more striking.

Waterfall in Norway was probably painted in the late 1660s or early 1670s, when van Ruisdael returned once more to the theme that had captured his fancy. In the present painting the earlier sense of tension is replaced by a classical clarity. This change is evident in the transition to a horizontal format allowing a broad range of space, in the precise articulation of planes, and in the signs he provides of human habitation: it is not by chance that a peasant house sits on the rocky rise beside the waterfall and an idyllic figure of a shepherd is seen on the riverbank. The staffage in this painting is traditionally attributed to Adriaen van de Velde (1636–1672), in which case the work could not have been painted after 1672, the year of van de Velde's death.

In addition to this canvas van Ruisdael painted several landscapes of similar composition in the early 1670s. They are in the Wallace Collection, London; in the Rijksmuseum, Amsterdam; and in a private collection in London.

PROVENANCE: Acquired by the Hermitage in 1769 from the Brühl collection, Dresden
HERMITAGE CATALOGUES: 1774, no. 1417; 1863–1916, no. 1145; 1958, II, p. 250; 1981, p. 163
EXHIBITIONS: 1968–69 Belgrade, no. 34; 1985 Rotterdam, no. 26, p. 142
LITERATURE: Livret 1838, I, no. 18; Somov 1859, p. 113; Waagen 1864, p. 244; Bode 1873, p. 39; Benois [1910], p. 420; Wurzbach 1910, II, p. 520; Hofstede de Groot 1911, IV, no. 276; Rosenberg 1928, no. 178; Fechner 1958, p. 19; Fechner 1963, p. 94; Kuznetsov 1973, p. 35; Slive and Hoetink 1981, p. 107; Tarasov 1983, p. 224

IS

MATTHIAS STOMER (STOM)

ca. 1600 Amersfoort–ca. 1650 Sicily(?)
Influenced by Gerrit van Honthorst and the later works of Caravaggio.
Lived in Rome (ca. 1630), Naples, and perhaps Sicily.

31. *Esau Selling His Birthright*
    Oil on canvas, 46½ × 64⅝ in. (118 × 164 cm.)
    Inv. no. 2913

Dutch Caravaggism had many fine representatives, among them Gerrit van Honthorst, Hendrik ter Brugghen, and Dirk van Baburen. Matthias Stomer occupies a place apart in this movement, rejecting humorous genre scenes and elaborate decorative allegories in favor of scenes from the Old and New Testaments. The present painting is based on Genesis 25:29–34.

Stomer was an outstanding master. It would be difficult to find a work in which the flickering light from a candle flame is conveyed with such rich tonal effects as in his *Esau Selling His Birthright*. And how telling is the encounter of five hands in the center of the composition, which allows the viewer to sense the source of the conflict. This work was painted in the 1640s.

It was formerly attributed to Honthorst, but a reattribution to Stomer, made by Shcherbacheva (1964), has been confirmed by comparison with many other paintings by the artist, particularly a quite similar version of the Hermitage work in the Staatliche Museen, Berlin-Dahlem. A second version, in a very poor state of preservation, is in the Gilberto Algranti collection, Milan.

PROVENANCE: Acquired by the Hermitage in 1915 from the P. P. Semenov-Tianshansky collection, Petrograd
HERMITAGE CATALOGUES: 1958, II, p. 272; 1981, p. 170
EXHIBITIONS: 1973 Leningrad, no. 56

LITERATURE: Semenov 1885, I, p. 232; Semenov 1906, no. 222 (as Honthorst); Semenov 1906b, p. XXXVIII; Shcherbacheva 1964, pp. 24–26; Vsevolozhskaya and Linnik 1975, nos. 146–48; Nicolson 1977, pp. 239, 242; Nicolson 1979, p. 93

IL

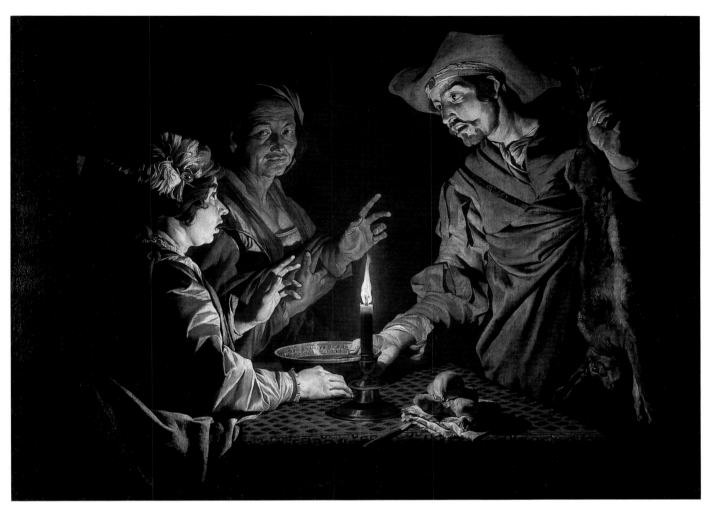

31

WILLEM VAN DE VELDE THE YOUNGER

1633 Leiden–1707 London
Studied with his father, Willem van de Velde the Elder, in Amsterdam, then
with Simon de Vlieger in Weesp. Worked in Amsterdam (until 1672).
Accompanied the Dutch fleet during the war with France and England.
Went with his father to England (1672), where both entered the service of the
Stuart kings Charles II and James II. Painted marine scenes.

32. *Ships in the Roads*
Oil on canvas (transferred to a new canvas in 1893), 42 × 48 in.
  (106.7 × 121.9 cm.)
Signed and dated lower right: W.v.Velde 1653
Inv. no. 1021

This early work by van de Velde depicts sailing and rowing vessels becalmed at
sea. In the center is a royal yacht with a tall, richly adorned stern bearing the
coat of arms of the House of Orange.

   The picture belongs to the type of seascape often painted by Simon
de Vlieger and Jan van de Cappelle in the mid-seventeenth century. Van de
Velde enlivens the subject by introducing a bathing scene in the foreground.
His rendering of the moisture-laden air is masterly, and the sense of peacefulness
is intensified by the rhythmic placement of the sails and their reflections in the
water. Works such as this, painted in a bright palette, earned the artist great
popularity in the eighteenth century.

PROVENANCE: Acquired by the Hermitage
in 1770 from the Tronchin collection, Geneva
HERMITAGE CATALOGUES: 1774, no. 426;
1863–1916, no. 1185; 1958, II, p. 150; 1981,
p. 114
EXHIBITIONS: 1972 Dresden, no. 47; 1974
Geneva, no. 257

LITERATURE: Waagen 1864, p. 251; Clément
de Ris 1879, II, p. 387; Benois [1910], p. 415;
Wurzbach 1910, II, p. 757; Willis [1911],
p. 83; Hofstede de Groot 1915, VII, no. 92;
Fechner 1963, pp. 145, 146, 173, ills. 102,
104; Stechow 1966, p. 120. pl. 239; Levinson-
Lessing 1970, p. 12, no. 77; Bol 1973, p. 233

IS

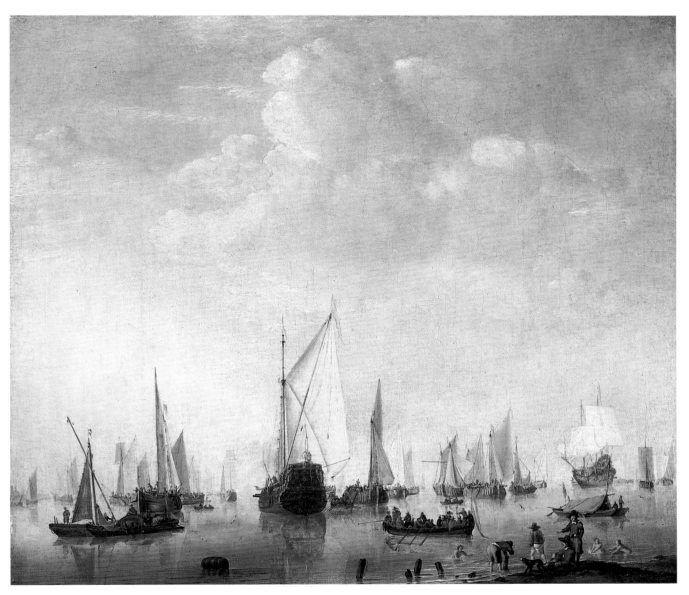

32

71

EMANUEL DE WITTE

ca. 1614 Alkmaar–1692 Amsterdam
Studied with still-life painter Evert van Aelst. Influenced by Gerrit Houckgeest and Hendrick van Vliet. Lived in Rotterdam (1639–40), Delft (ca. 1641–51), and Amsterdam (ca. 1652). Painted church interiors, genre scenes, and mythological subjects, as well as portraits and harbor and market scenes.

33. *A Protestant Gothic Church*
Oil on canvas, 31½ × 26 in. (80 × 66 cm.)
Traces of a signature lower left: E.DE . . .
Inv. no. 803

Here the nave and the transept are seen from the south aisle. At the right is the pulpit, where a preacher stands. The congregation fills the space between the tall columns, beyond which is the organ with open shutters.

Like a series of mature works by de Witte, the present painting combines motifs taken from two Amsterdam churches, the Oude Kerk and the Nieuwe Kerk. As Manke (1963) has noted, de Witte freely combines architectural elements from actual interiors, much as a landscape painter adapts his sketches from nature in the studio. By using this method de Witte succeeds in making an imaginary interior extraordinarily convincing. A sense of depth is captured not only through the use of linear perspective but also through the masterly distribution of patches of sunlight. The geometric pattern thus formed on the columns and walls creates a feeling of light and air. The soaring space, pierced by a dynamic stream of sunlight, and the sharp contrasts of light and shadow make a strong emotional impression.

The painting has been variously dated. In the catalogue of the François Tronchin collection, where it remained until 1770, it is said to carry a date of 1671, though no traces of such a date have survived. However, a similar composition in a private collection is dated 1669 (reproduced in Liedtke 1982, pl. XIII). Manke (1963) places the Hermitage work in the period around 1685.

PROVENANCE: Acquired by the Hermitage in 1770 from the Tronchin collection, Geneva; transferred in the nineteenth century to the Gatchina Palace; returned to the Hermitage in 1924
HERMITAGE CATALOGUES: 1774, no. 551; 1958, II, p. 162; 1981, p. 122

EXHIBITIONS: 1974 Geneva, no. 291; 1977 Tokyo–Kyoto, no. 25; 1981 Madrid, p. 62
LITERATURE: Jantzen 1910, p. 177, no. 687; Shchavinsky 1916, p. 75; Manke 1963, p. 101, no. 99; Levinson-Lessing 1964, no. 53; Levinson-Lessing 1970, p. 10, no. 46

IS

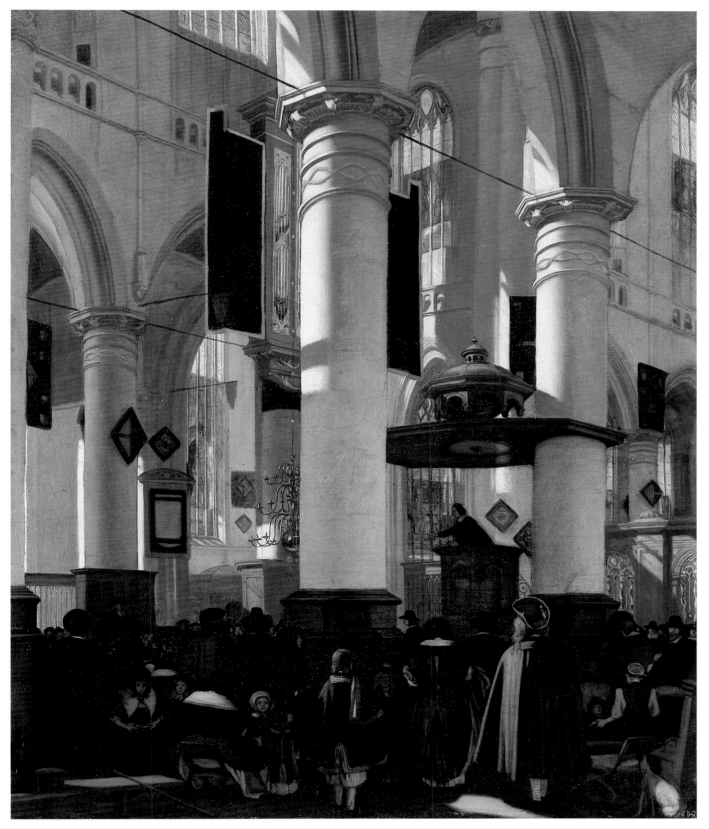

33

JOACHIM WTTEWAEL

ca. 1566 Utrecht–1638 Utrecht
Studied with his father Antonie Wttewael, a glass painter, and Joost de Beer.
Worked in Utrecht (from 1611 member of the painters' guild). Visited Italy
(1587–92). Painted religious, mythological, and genre subjects and also
portraits.

34. *The Baptism of Christ*
Oil on canvas, 36¼ × 57⅝ in. (92 × 146.5 cm.)
Inv. no. 5187

The great social changes that took place in the United Provinces after independence had been achieved were not immediately felt in the art of the Dutch
republic. The Mannerist tradition lasted well into the seventeenth century,
and the Utrecht painter Joachim Wttewael belonged to the last generation of
Dutch Mannerists. His painting differs from that of the Haarlem Mannerists
Henrik Goltzius and Cornelis van Haarlem primarily in its brighter and more
varied palette. In *The Baptism of Christ* the principal scene has been placed far
to the back of the composition, while the entire foreground is occupied by a
crowd of spectators in mannered poses. The clear reds, blues, and yellows of
their clothing create a festive and elegant spectacle. Loewenthal (1982) dates the
picture to about 1618–24.

PROVENANCE: Acquired by the Hermitage
in 1926 through the State Museum Fund
HERMITAGE CATALOGUES: 1958, II, p. 286;
1981, p. 186

LITERATURE: Loewenthal 1982, pp. 145–46,
no. A80, pl. III

IL

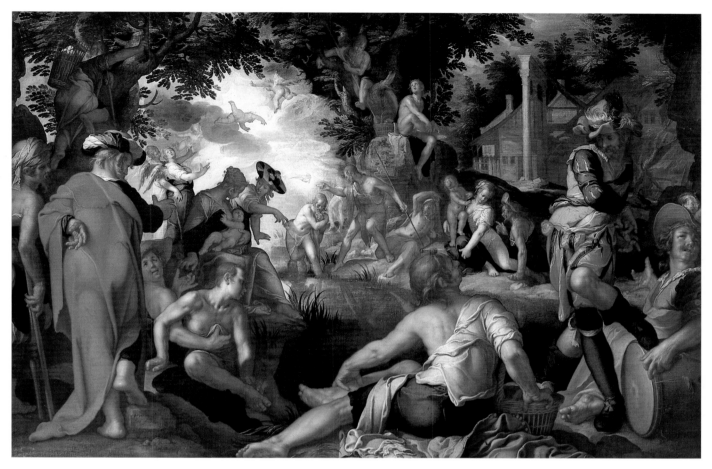

34

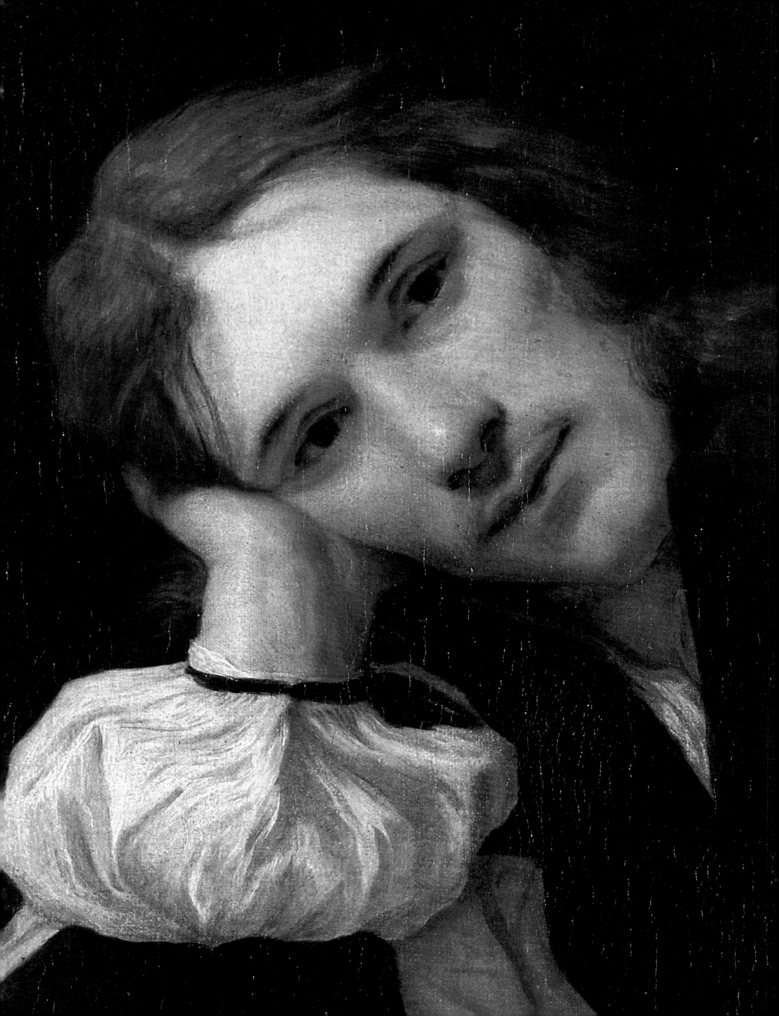

FLEMISH PAINTINGS
OF THE
SEVENTEENTH
CENTURY

◁ Detail: Plate 50

JAN BRUEGHEL I

1568 Brussels—1625 Antwerp
Younger son of Pieter Brueghel the Elder. Pupil of Pieter Goetkint and
possibly of Gillis van Coninxloo. Called Velvet-, Flowers-, and Paradise-
Brueghel. As a young man visited Cologne; later spent many years in Italy,
working in Naples (1590), Rome (1593–94), and Milan (1595–96), where he
entered the service of the Archbishop of Milan, Federigo Borromeo. On
return from Italy settled in Antwerp, where he lived until his death (from
1597 a master of the Guild of Saint Luke; in 1601–2 dean of the guild). Went
to Prague (1604); traveled to Holland with Rubens and Hendrik van Balen
(ca. 1613). Became court painter to the rulers of the Spanish Netherlands,
Archduke Albert and Archduchess Isabella (1609). Collaborated with Rubens
and other artists. Painted landscapes, still lifes,and animals, as well as
religious, mythological, and allegorical subjects.

35. *Edge of a Forest (The Flight into Egypt)*
Oil on copper, 9⅞ × 14⅛ in. (25 × 36 cm.)
Signed and dated lower left: BRVeghel 1610
Inv. no. 429

One of the landscape motifs Brueghel liked to paint was the forest thicket or
the forest edge. These paintings had their origin in the forest scenes of Gillis
van Coninxloo (1544–1607), the initiator of the forest landscape in Western
European painting. But in contrast to the romantic, somewhat gloomy atmosphere that pervades Coninxloo's landscapes, Brueghel's works have a serene
character. The world he creates has an enchanted atmosphere, devoid of storms
and passions and softly lyrical in mood. In accordance with tradition Brueghel
incorporates scenes from the Bible in his landscapes, but he treats them by and
large as genre or narrative scenes. The figures in the Hermitage painting,
which shows the Holy Family's Flight into Egypt (Matthew 2:13–15), are treated
as if they were part of an episode Brueghel had observed in everyday life.

The authenticity of the painting's signature and execution has not been
questioned by experts, with the exception of Ertz (1979), who without any
evidence considers it a forgery. The painting has all the hallmarks of Brueghel's
mature style: the soft harmony of bright, radiant colors, the precise draftsman-
ship, and the virtuoso finesse with which he paints the smallest details. The
donkey in the figural group in the foreground is taken almost unchanged from
the study of a donkey in the center of his *Animal Studies* (Kunsthistorisches
Museum, Vienna).

A copy of the Hermitage work, attributed to Pieter Gysels, was in a sale
at the P. de Boer Gallery, Amsterdam, in spring 1965 (no. 31, oil on copper,
11¼ × 16¾ in. [28.5 × 42.5 cm.]).

PROVENANCE: Acquired by the Hermitage
in 1772 from the Crozat collection, Paris
HERMITAGE CATALOGUES: 1774, no. 872;
1863–1916, no. 520; 1958, II, p. 39; 1981,
p. 34

EXHIBITIONS: 1978 Leningrad, no. 3
LITERATURE: Crozat 1755, p. 80; Somov
1859, p. 105; Waagen 1864; Semenov 1885,
I, pp. 106–7, 326; Benois [1910], p. 258;
Thiery 1953, p. 176; Ertz 1979, p. 232

NG

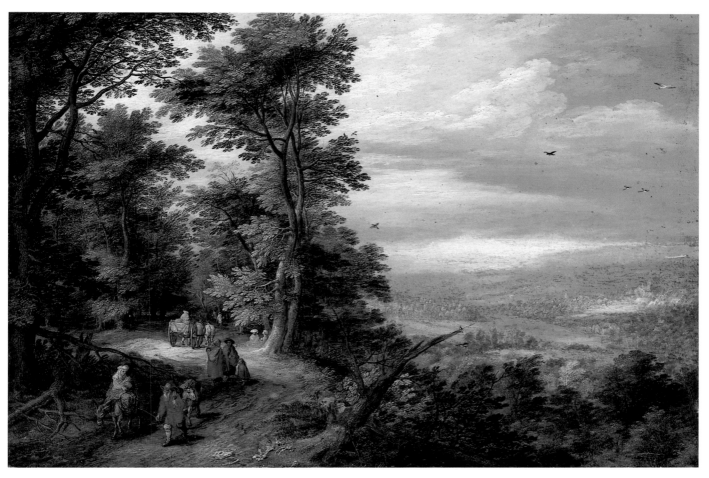

35

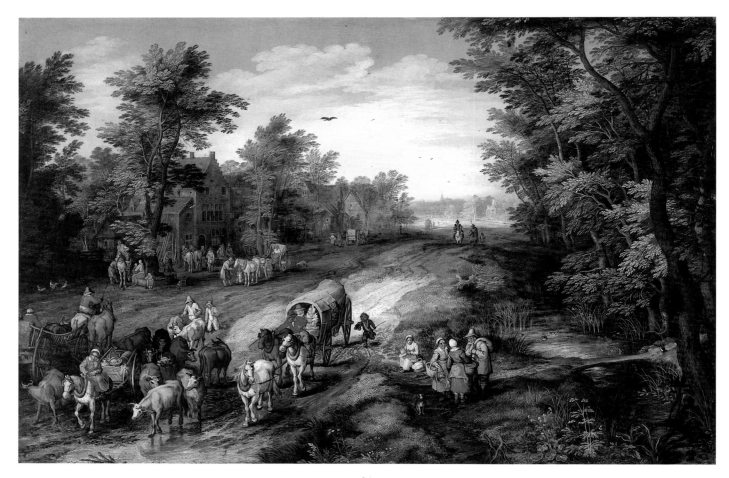

36

JAN BRUEGHEL I

36. *Village Street*
Oil on copper, 10 × 15 in. (25.5 × 38 cm.)
Inv. no. 430

This painting belongs to a large group of landscape works by Brueghel that have as their subject vignettes from everyday life in village streets. Although they were probably inspired by one of his father's graphic series depicting simple village scenes (for example, *Praediorum villarum*, a series of engravings published by I. Kok), they were always based on sketches from nature made during Brueghel's travels and his long walks in the environs of Antwerp.

The Hermitage work is based on Brueghel's drawing *The Forest Path* (Staatliche Museen, Berlin-Dahlem), which depicts an actual place. Brueghel then transforms his direct impressions into a bright, fairy-tale world as he strives for his unique velvety surface. It was this surface quality that confirmed his nickname Velvet-Brueghel, originally coined by his contemporaries because of his passion for wearing expensive clothing.

The painting was apparently executed about 1611, since it appears to be a copy by Brueghel of an analogous composition, dated 1611, in a private collection in Utrecht (reproduced in Ertz 1979, no. 232). Another copy by the artist is in the Wellington Museum, London. Two other versions are known: one, dated 1610, was in the Stern Gallery, Düsseldorf, in 1936 (reproduced in Ertz 1979, no. 222); the other was in the Alte Pinakothek, Munich, until 1939 (reproduced in Winner 1961, p. 213, ill. 23).

PROVENANCE: Acquired by the Hermitage in 1769 from the Brühl collection, Dresden HERMITAGE CATALOGUES: 1774, no. 524; 1863–1916, no. 516; 1958, II, p. 40; 1981, p. 34

EXHIBITIONS: 1978 Leningrad, no. 4 LITERATURE: Livret 1838, p. 14, no. 33; Waagen 1864, p. 128; Semenov 1885, I, p. 106; Ertz 1979, p. 598, no. 242

NG

ANTHONY VAN DYCK

1599 Antwerp–1641 London
A pupil of Hendrik van Balen. Worked in Rubens's studio (1616/17–20).
Traveled to England (1620–21). Worked in Italy, primarily in Genoa and
Rome (1622–27). Returned to Antwerp (late 1627). Moved to London by
April 1, 1632, where he became court painter to Charles I; visited Antwerp
(1634, 1640, and 1641). Painted portraits and religious and mythological
subjects.

37. *Family Portrait*
Oil on canvas, 44¾ × 36⅞ in. (113.5 × 93.5 cm.)
Inv. no. 534

Of the numerous paintings of this type by van Dyck, the present work is one
of the most heartfelt. He succeeded magnificently in capturing the atmosphere
of warmth and cordiality that existed within his family. Attempts by scholars
(Waagen 1864, Cust 1900, Rosenbaum 1928) to identify the sitters as Frans
Snyders or Jan Wildens and their families were rejected after the Hermitage
painting was compared with authenticated portraits of these two Flemish painters
by van Dyck himself (cf. *Frans Snyders,* Schloss Wilhelmshöhe, Kassel, and
Frick Collection, New York, and *Jan Wildens*, Detroit Institute of Arts). Moreover, Snyders had no children.

An X-ray has revealed that the man's collar was repainted. Originally it
was a large millstone type whose outlines are still visible. Van Dyck may have
made the change to avoid overloading the upper part of the composition.

The canvas was painted at the end of 1621, just before van Dyck's departure for Italy. Two copies exist: one is in the Staatsgalerie, Stuttgart; the other is
in the Franklin Friementhal collection, England.

PROVENANCE: Acquired by the Hermitage
before 1774; previously in the La Live de
Jully collection, Paris
HERMITAGE CATALOGUES: 1774, no. 881;
1863–1916, no. 627; 1958, p. 52; 1981, p. 38
EXHIBITIONS: 1910 Brussels, no. 117; 1938
Leningrad, no. 33; 1967 Montreal, no. 65;
1972 Leningrad, no. 331; 1975–76 Washington, D.C., no. 17; 1978 Leningrad, no. 9;
1980 Ottawa, no. 72; 1981 Vienna, pp. 34–37;
1985 Rotterdam, no. 32
LITERATURE: Lalive 1764, p. 114; Schnitzler
1828, p. 103; Smith 1831, III, p. 28, no. 300;
Smith 1842, IX, p. 382, no. 51; Blanc 1857,
I, p. 165; Waagen 1864, p. 149; Guiffrey
1882, p. 112; Bode 1889, p. 46; Neustroyev
1898, p. 185; Cust 1900, pp. 18, 236, no. 56;
Rooses 1904, p. 116; Benois [1910], p. 251;
Dumont-Wilden 1910, p. 15; Heidrich 1913,
p. 73; Bode 1921, p. 350; Drost 1926, p. 64;
Rosenbaum 1928, p. 34; Glück 1931, pl.
108; Bazin [1958], p. 152; Varchavskaya 1963,
pp. 100, 101; Levinson-Lessing 1964, no. 15;
Larsen 1980, no. 128; Brown 1982, p. 50,
pl. 41; Gritsai 1982, p. 8, pl. 1; Millar 1982,
p. 12

NB

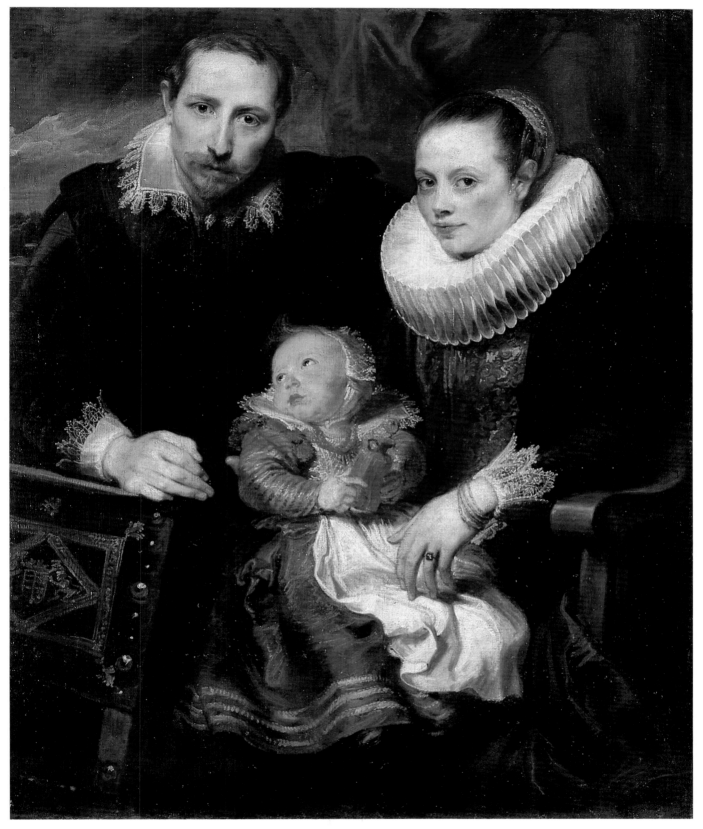

37

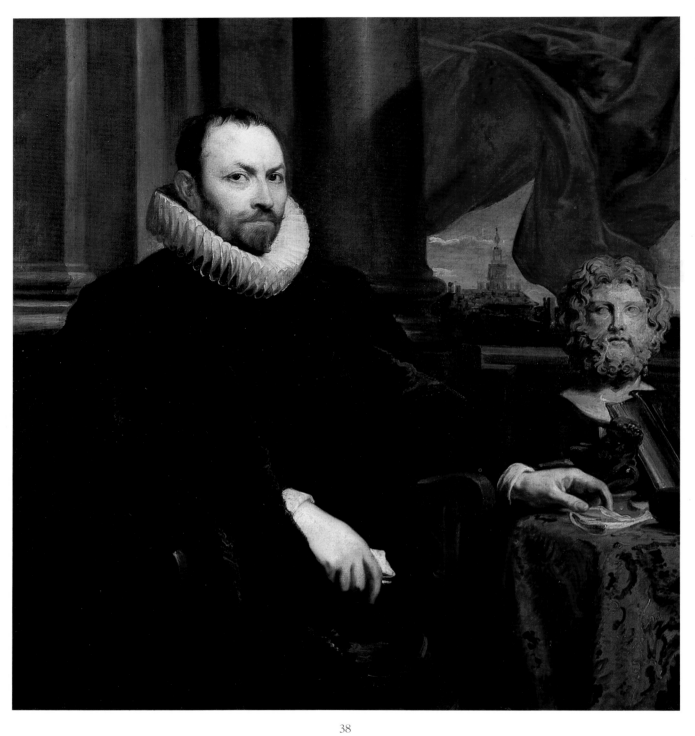

ANTHONY VAN DYCK

38. *Nicolaes Rockox*
Oil on canvas, 50⅜ × 46⅛ in. (128 × 117.3 cm.), including strips
added later to top (⅝ in. [1.5 cm.]) and bottom (1⅝ in. [4 cm.])
Inv. no. 6929

Nicolaes Rockox (1560–1640) was a numismatist, a collector, and from 1603 to 1636 the burgomaster of Antwerp. His identity is based primarily on an engraving by Lucas Vorsterman (Le Blanc, IV, p. 156, no. 72).

Rockox is shown in his study. Through the window can be seen the tower of the Hanseatic building in Antwerp, where the burgomaster evidently conducted business and which is as much an attribute of his activities as the books and the antique sculptures. In van Dyck's painting a marble bust of Plato(?) stands on the table, whereas in Vorsterman's engraving the bust is of Demosthenes. This difference can most likely be explained by the fact that Rockox did not acquire the bust of Demosthenes until after van Dyck had painted his portrait; Vorsterman then included it in his engraving (executed between 1622 and 1624) at the sitter's request.

A preparatory drawing for the Hermitage portrait is in London (reproduced in Hind 1923, 2, p. 60, no. 30; oval format, showing only the head). Several scholars (Hind 1923; Hulst and Vey 1960) attribute it to van Dyck, while others (Glück 1931) consider it to be a copy.

PROVENANCE: Transferred to the Hermitage in 1932 from the Stroganov Palace Museum, Leningrad. Mentioned as no. 4 in the posthumous inventory of Rockox's possessions of December 19/20, 1640 (Cuyck 1881). According to Hoet (1752) the painting appeared at the Anna Theresa van Halen auction in Antwerp, August 19, 1748, and in the Frederico van Toms auction in Leiden, April 7, 1750. It was listed in the latter sale as *Portrait of an Antwerp Burgomaster* and attributed to Rubens (the only instance of confusion over van Dyck's authorship of this painting). Mariette (1853–54) claims that in the eighteenth century the portrait was in the Vetellier collection in Paris. It was acquired by Count A. S. Stroganov between 1769 and 1779, during his stay in Paris (manuscript preserved in the Hermitage; J. Schmidt, *Burgermeister Rockox*, 1931)

HERMITAGE CATALOGUES: 1958, p. 52; 1981, p. 39

LITERATURE: Hoet 1752, p. 256, no. 1, p. 282, no. 2; Stroganoff 1793, no. 34; Stroganoff 1800, no. 45; Smith 1831, III, p. 86; Mariette 1853–54, II, p. 207; Waagen 1864, p. 404; Cuyck 1881, pp. 339–451; Michiels 1881, pp. 228–32; Guiffrey 1882, p. 276; Cust 1900, pp. 17, 234, no. 27; Bode 1921, pp. 348, 361; Hind 1923, p. 60; Glück 1931, p. 530, note 110; Delacre 1934, pp. 23–30; Hendrick 1939, pp. 67–110; Bazin [1958], p. 240; Hulst and Vey 1960, pp. 144, 145; Gerson and Kuile 1960, pp. 115, 190; Varchavskaya 1963, pp. 101, 105; Larsen 1980, no. 295; Brown 1982, pp. 57–59, pl. 46

NB

ANTHONY VAN DYCK

39. *Self-portrait*
Oil on canvas, 45⅞ × 36⅞ in. (116.5 × 93.5 cm.)
Inv. no. 548

In the course of his life van Dyck painted several self-portraits. One of his first works, painted at a very early age, was a portrait of himself (Akademie der Bildenden Künste, Vienna).

The present self-portrait is one of three similar works painted at different periods and apparently based on a single study, which has not survived. The other versions are in the Alte Pinakothek, Munich, and The Metropolitan Museum of Art, New York.

Stylistic and technological evidence suggests that the present painting was executed not earlier than the late 1620s or early 1630s. It is certainly the latest of the three versions. Van Dyck was older than he portrayed himself here, and he apparently wished to create an idealized representation of himself. His elegant pose, the picturesque disarray of his clothing, and the romantic setting (the broken column and the twilit sky) are in accord with the youthful charm of his face with its dreamy expression and its halo of golden curls.

When van Dyck painted the present portrait, he was already a celebrated artist and the creator of a type of aristocratic portrait that remained a standard in Western Europe for many years. Here he endows his own image with aristocratic features, stressing the elegance of his figure and his well-groomed hands with their long, slender fingers.

The portrait was engraved by J. van der Brugghen in 1682 (Le Blanc, I, p. 530, no. 15) and by S. Silvestre (1694–1738; Le Blanc, III, p. 516, no. 2); the latter shows only the head.

A copy of the portrait is in the Devonshire collection, Chatsworth.

PROVENANCE: Acquired by the Hermitage in 1772 from the Crozat collection, Paris
HERMITAGE CATALOGUES: 1774, no. 1025; 1863–1916, no. 628; 1958, II, p. 56; 1981, p. 39
EXHIBITIONS: 1938 Leningrad, no. 36; 1972 Leningrad, no. 333; 1972 Moscow, pp. 51, 62; 1978 Leningrad, no. 12; 1980 Ottawa, no. 77; 1981 Vienna, pp. 38–41; 1983 Tokyo, no. "A"; 1985 Rotterdam, no. 33
LITERATURE: Crozat 1755, p. 7; Livret 1838, p. 361; Smith 1842, IX, p. 395, no. 98; Waagen 1864, p. 150; Cust 1900, p. 233, no. 42; Glück 1931, pl. 122; Glück 1934, p. 195; Puyvelde 1950, pp. 96, 125, 130; Speth-Holterhoff 1957, p. 25; Gerson and Kuile 1960, p. 121; Varchavskaya 1963, pp. 110–12; Levinson-Lessing 1964, no. 17; Stuffmann 1968, p. 96; Larsen 1980, no. 256; Brown 1982, p. 52; Gritsai 1982, p. 8, pl. 4; Millar 1982, p. 15; Broos 1986, pp. 160, 161

NB

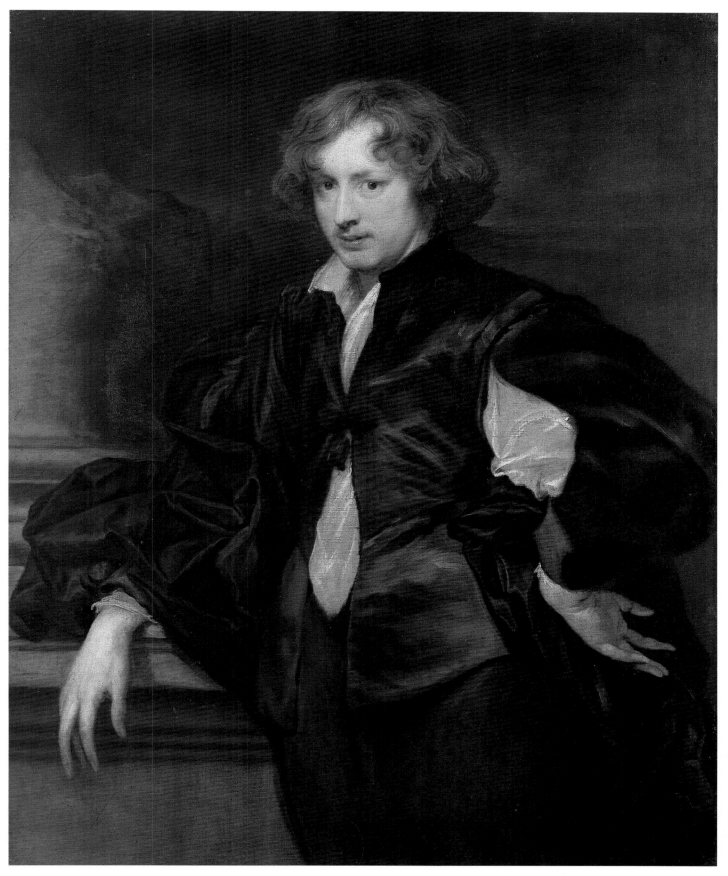

39

ANTHONY VAN DYCK

40. *Henry Danvers, Earl of Danby*
Oil on canvas, 87¾ × 51⅜ in. (223 × 130.6 cm.)
Inv. no. 545

Henry Danvers (1573–1644), Earl of Danby and Knight of the Order of the Garter (1633), took part in military campaigns in France, Flanders, and Ireland. It was probably in one such campaign that he received the wound on his left temple, whose scar is here covered by a dark patch. Danvers founded the first botanical garden in England, at Oxford.

A stylistic analysis of the painting shows a lack of uniformity in the brushwork, which suggests that only the head was painted by van Dyck, with the clothing and accessories being painted by his assistants.

The portrait was painted in the late 1630s. It was engraved by V. Green for the Walpole collection in 1788.

There is a preparatory drawing in the British Museum, London (reproduced in Hind 1923, p. 68, no. 57). Glück (1931) cites two copies of the portrait: one in the Stamford collection at Denham Massey, England, the other in the collection at Wentworth Castle, England.

PROVENANCE: Acquired by the Hermitage in 1779 from the Walpole collection, Houghton Hall, England; was earlier a gift from Sir Joseph Danvers to Robert Walpole
HERMITAGE CATALOGUES: 1863–1916, no. 615; 1958, II, p. 60; 1981, p. 40
EXHIBITIONS: 1982–83 London, no. 20
LITERATURE: Aedes Walpolianae 1752, p. 72; Schnitzler 1828, p. 103; Smith 1831, III, p. 188, no. 647; Livret 1838, p. 350; Smith 1842, IX, p. 394, no. 92; Waagen 1864, p. 151; Guiffrey 1882, p. 264; Neustroyev 1898, p. 183; Cust 1900, p. 124, 273, no. 61; Rooses 1904, p. 115; Benois [1910], p. 252; Hind 1923, p. 68; Glück 1931, pl. 247; Bazin [1958], p. 152; Varchavskaya 1963, p. 127; Larsen 1980, no. 934; Millar 1982, p. 62, no. 20

NB

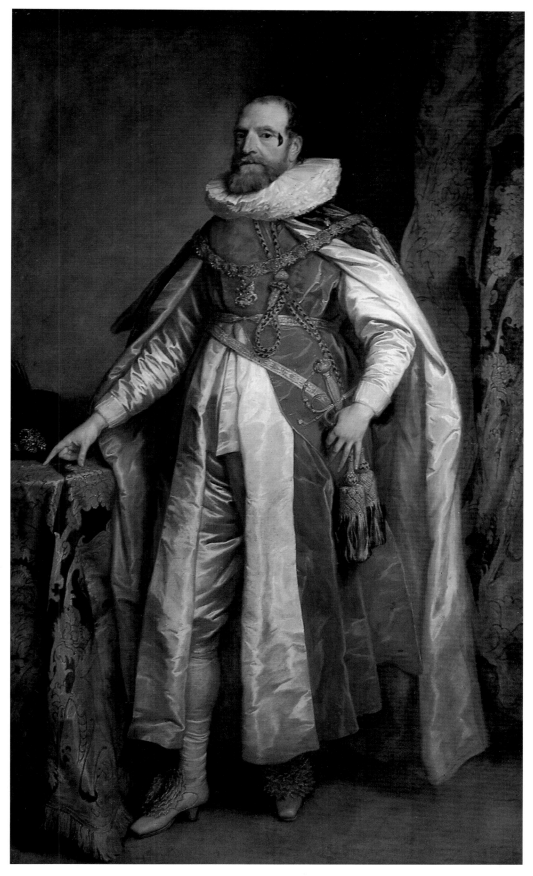

40

JAN FYT

1611 Antwerp—1661 Antwerp
Studied with Hans van den Berch (1620–21), then worked in the studio of
Frans Snyders. Became a master of the Antwerp Guild of Saint Luke (1629).
After 1631 spent a long period traveling; lived and worked in Paris
(1633–34), Venice, and Rome. Returned to Antwerp in 1641. Painted still
lifes and animals.

41. *Hare, Fruit, and Parrot*
    Oil on canvas, 27¾ × 38¼ in. (70.5 × 97 cm.)
    Signed and dated lower left on sheet of paper: Joannes Fyt 1647
    Inv. no. 616

Unlike his teacher Snyders, who always emphasized the plastic, sensuous qualities of objects, Fyt approached the still life as a specific painterly problem.
Although, as a true Flemish painter, he conscientiously rendered the plastic
values of forms, his attention was focused on the search for subtle color combi-
nations and refined decorative effects. Fyt captured with far greater subtlety
than Snyders the different textures of each of the objects he painted. In the
present painting he juxtaposes the soft, fluffy golden-brown fur of the hare,
the white of the tablecloth, and the silky pearl-gray plumage of the partridge.
While Snyders usually constructed his still lifes on an equilibrium of broad
color patches and often used wide planes of saturated red as a foundation for
his color composition, Fyt avoided large planes of bright color. The composition of the Hermitage still life is based on a delicate harmony of olive, gray,
brown, and yellowish tones, enlivened by small red, green, and blue patches.

The central motif in this painting was repeated by Fyt in *Still Life: Hare,
Partridges, and Fruit* (Metropolitan Museum, New York), which is a greatly
amplified version of the Hermitage work.

PROVENANCE: Acquired by the Hermitage
before 1774; from the late eighteenth century
was in the Hermitage pavilion in Peterhof;
returned to the Hermitage in 1921
HERMITAGE CATALOGUES: 1774, no. 457;
1958, II, p. 110; 1981, p. 77

EXHIBITIONS: 1983 Dresden, no. 64; 1984
Leningrad—Moscow, no. 105; 1985
Rotterdam, no. 34
LITERATURE: Waagen 1864, p. 364;
Levinson-Lessing 1926, p. 36

NG

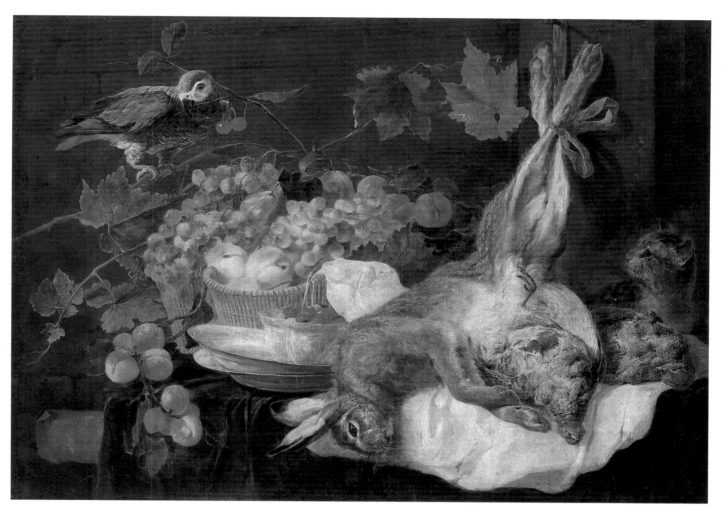

41

JACOB JORDAENS

1593 Antwerp–1678 Antwerp
Apprenticed in 1607 to the Antwerp painter Adam van Noort, who was also
Rubens's teacher. In 1615 became a master of the Antwerp Guild of Saint
Luke, specializing in tempera, gouache, and watercolor (dean of the guild,
1621–22). In 1616 married van Noort's eldest daughter, Catharina. Lived and
worked in Antwerp. Converted to Calvinism in the 1650s but continued to
accept commissions from Catholic churches and monasteries. Painted
religious, mythological, historical, and allegorical subjects, as well as portraits
and genre scenes.

42. *Self-portrait with Parents, Brothers, and Sisters*
Oil on canvas, 69 × 54⅛ in. (175.2 × 137.5 cm.)
Inv. no. 484

This portrait was long believed to show Jordaens surrounded by his own family or by the family of his teacher and father-in-law, Adam van Noort. Held
(1940) established that it actually portrays the artist's parents—the Antwerp
linen merchant Jacob Jordaens and his wife, Barbara van Wolschaten—the
artist himself, holding a lute, and seven of his brothers and sisters. In the
foreground are the twin brothers, Abraham and Isaac (b. 1606), while the little
girl on her mother's lap is apparently Elizabeth (b. 1613). The young woman to
the left of her mother is probably Maria (b. 1596), and near her is Anna
(b. 1597). The girl peeping out from behind her mother's shoulder may be
Catharina (b. 1600); and finally, the child to the right of the father appears to
be Magdalena (b. 1608). Jordaens's parents had three more children: Anna
(b. 1595), Elizabeth (b. 1605), and Suzanna (b. 1610), all of whom evidently died
in infancy. True to Netherlandish tradition, the figures hovering above the
group personify the souls of these children.

Based on this identification, the portrait can be dated to about 1615 and
is thus one of Jordaens's earliest known group portraits. It was possibly painted
to commemorate Jordaens's acceptance as a master by the Guild of Saint Luke
and perhaps depicts the family's celebration of this event. Here Jordaens used
a type of multifigure composition, common in Netherlandish painting from
the 1560s on, which shows the family grouped around a table with some of the
members playing musical instruments (cf. Frans Floris, *Van Berchem Family*,
1561, Museum Wuyts-Van Campen en Baron Caroly, Lier, and *The Moucheron
Family*, 1563, by an Amsterdam master, Rijksmuseum, Amsterdam). The composition of the Hermitage portrait was evidently inspired by Rubens's sketch
of about 1605 for an altarpiece depicting the Circumcision for the Church of
Sant'Ambrogio, Genoa (Akademie der Bildenden Künste, Vienna). Jordaens
could have seen the sketch in Rubens's studio, after Rubens brought it back
from Italy in 1608.

Jordaens's portrait was engraved by James Watson (under the title *Rubens
and His Family*) shortly before 1779 and lithographed by E. Guillot for Gohier-
Desfontains, *Galerie Impériale de l'Ermitage*, Saint Petersburg, 1845–47.

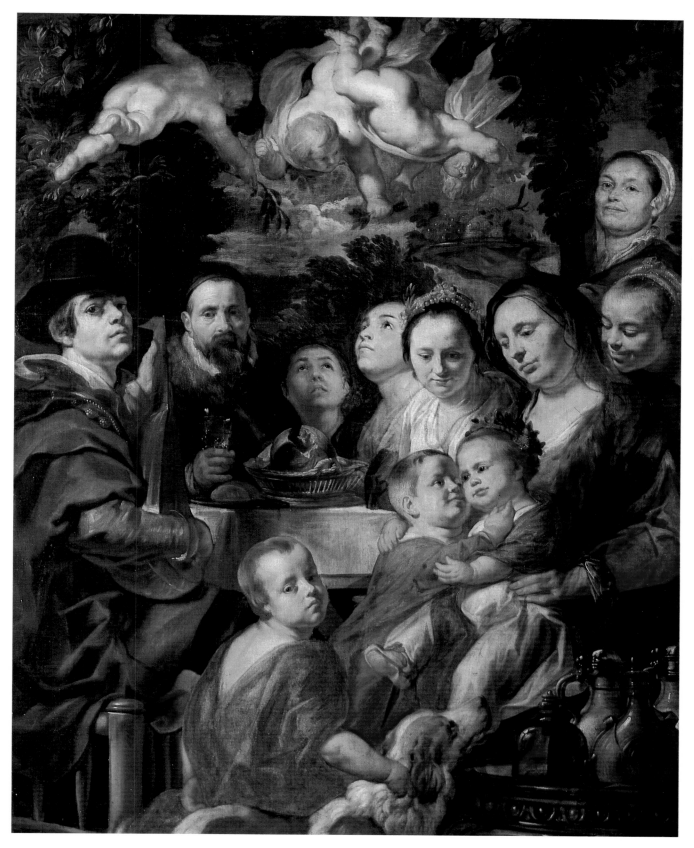

42

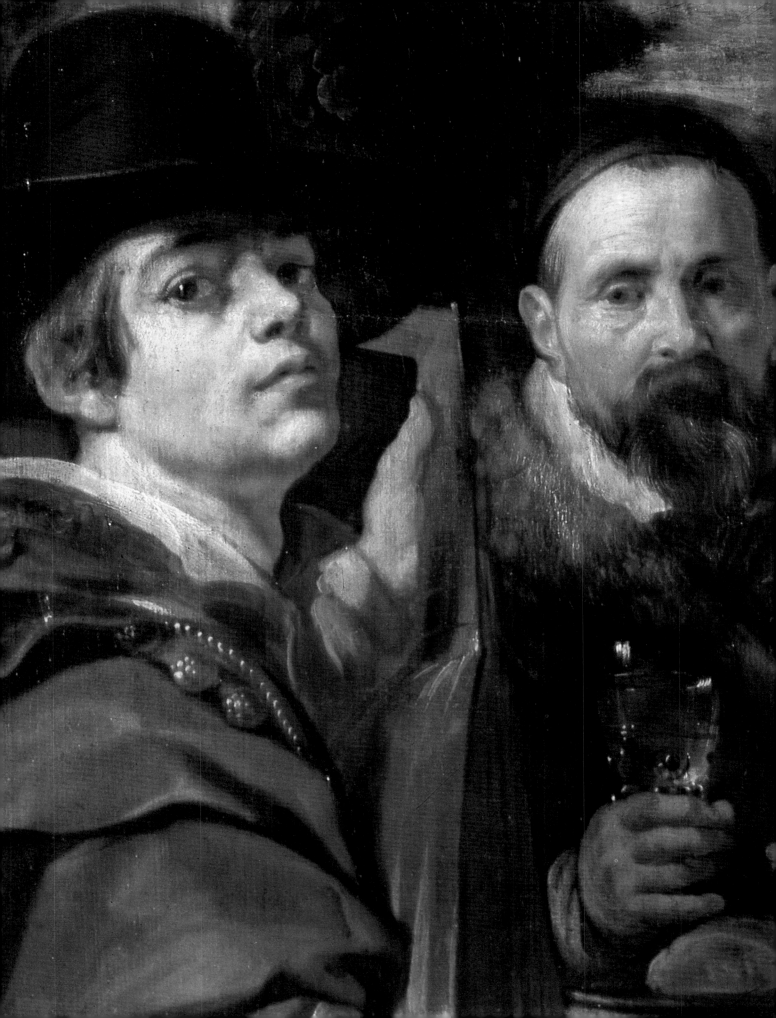

PROVENANCE: Acquired by the Hermitage in 1779 from the Walpole collection, Houghton Hall, England; previously in the collection of the Duke of Portland

HERMITAGE CATALOGUES: 1863–1916, no. 652; 1958, II, p. 65; 1981, p. 49

EXHIBITIONS: 1938 Leningrad, no. 60; 1968–69 Belgrade, no. 3; 1972 Leningrad, no. 339; 1977 Tokyo–Kyoto, no. 14; 1978 Leningrad, no. 15; 1979 Leningrad, no. 1; 1985 Rotterdam, no. 35

LITERATURE: Aedes Walpolianae 1752, p. 65; Livret 1838, p. 339; Waagen 1864, p. 155; Buschmann 1905, pp. 85–86; Rooses 1906, p. 54; Held 1940, pp. 70–82; Hulst 1956, p. 22; Jaffé 1969, p. 8, no. 3; Gritsai 1977, pp. 83–87; Held 1982, pp. 9–24; Hulst 1982, pp. 266, 268

NG

◁ Detail: Plate 42

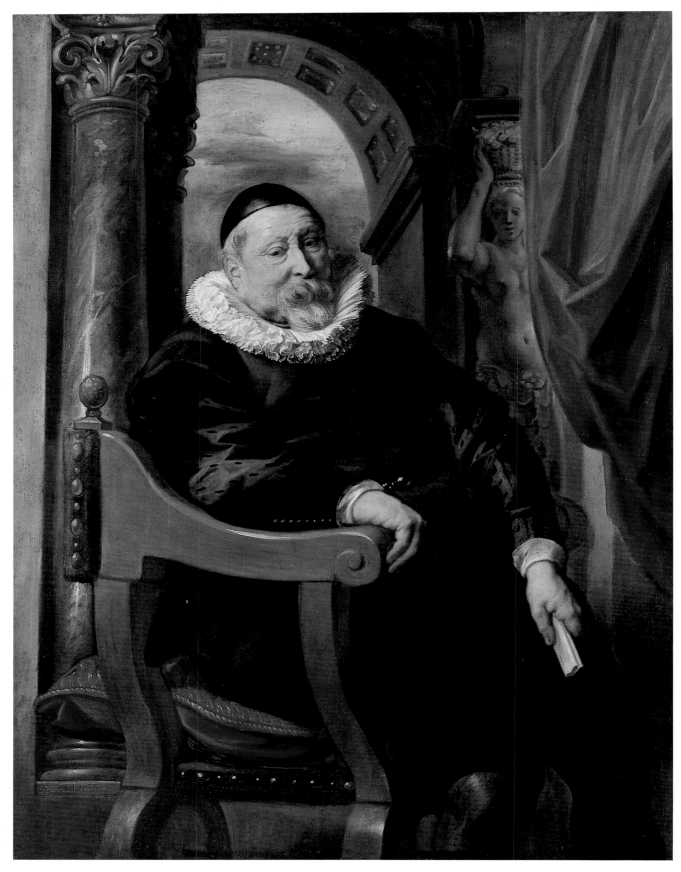

43

JACOB JORDAENS

43. *Portrait of an Old Man*

Oil on canvas, 60⅝ × 46⅝ in. (154 × 118.5 cm.)
Inscribed on column base at lower left: Aetatis 73
Inv. no. 486

Attempts to identify the sitter as either the Antwerp merchant Jacques van Lein or the painter Adam van Noort have been unsuccessful. *Portrait of an Old Man* is a companion piece to *Portrait of a Middle-Aged Lady* (Lord Farringdon collection, Bascott Park, England), which is inscribed "Aet. 66."

Portrait of an Old Man is typical of the numerous commissioned portraits that Jordaens painted during the 1630s and 1640s. In these works he drew on the whole repertoire of devices for creating a ceremonial, representational portrait which Rubens and van Dyck had so brilliantly developed: a magnificent architectural background, bright draperies, an elegant costume, and a low viewpoint that makes the sitter appear to be on a pedestal. But whereas van Dyck always strove in his ceremonial portraits to stress the sitter's inner nobility and the significance of his spiritual world and his aristocratic blood and spirit, Jordaens clearly wished to depict an actual social type—the prosperous bourgeois. In the Hermitage portrait he did not flatter his aged and corpulent sitter. Yet the architectural decor and the bulk of the figure, rendered in precise outlines and substantial forms, lend a grandeur to the image.

The portrait was painted before 1641, the date inscribed on a second version (Thyssen-Bornemisza Collection, Lugano), which also records the sitter's age as seventy-three. This second version is inferior to the present painting and appears to be a copy painted somewhat later, with minor alterations, in Jordaens's studio. A. N. Nemilov has commented (in conversation) that the Lugano portrait originally bore a different date: the number 37 is clearly discernible beneath the number 41. From this we may conclude that the sitter was seventy-three not in 1641, but in 1637, when he sat for Jordaens. The Hermitage portrait was evidently painted at the earlier date, a hypothesis borne out by the painting's style: the brushwork is identical to that of the Hermitage's *Feast of the Bean*, painted about 1638. The revised date of 1641 on the Lugano portrait probably refers to the year it was copied from the Hermitage original, and it may be that the sitter was no longer alive when the later work was commissioned. It should also be pointed out that the Hermitage portrait shows a much closer correspondence to a preparatory drawing than does the Lugano version.

PROVENANCE: Acquired by the Hermitage in 1772 from the Crozat collection, Paris
HERMITAGE CATALOGUES: 1774, no. 992; 1863–1916, no. 653; 1958, II, p. 65; 1981, p. 49
EXHIBITIONS: 1938 Leningrad, no. 61; 1972 Leningrad, no. 340; 1979 Leningrad, no. 6; 1985 Sapporo, no. 28

LITERATURE: Crozat 1775, p. 47; Livret 1838, p. 266; Waagen 1864, p. 156; Buschmann 1905, p. 101; Rooses 1906, p. 111; Puyvelde 1953, p. 131; Hulst 1956, pp. 190, 349, no. 72; Hulst 1974, p. 261; Gritsai 1977, pp. 88–91; Hulst 1982, p. 285

NG

PETER PAUL RUBENS

1577 Siegen (Westphalia)–1640 Antwerp

Son of Jan Rubens, an Antwerp lawyer who emigrated to Westphalia during the governor-generalship of the Duke of Alba. After his death in Cologne (1587) the family returned to Antwerp, where Peter Paul Rubens attended a Latin school. In 1591 began to study painting with Antwerp artists: first with Tobias Verhaecht, then with Adam van Noort, and finally with Otto van Veen. Lived in Italy (1600–1608), where he became court painter to the Duke of Mantua. Worked in Rome, Mantua, Genoa, and Venice. Appointed court painter to the Spanish rulers of the southern Netherlands, Archduke Albert and Archduchess Isabella. Lived in Antwerp (1609). Also involved in the diplomatic service. Traveled to Paris (1622–25), Holland (1627), Madrid (1628–29), and London (1629–30). On return from Italy became head of a large studio which for many years was the center of the country's artistic life. Received numerous commissions from all parts of Europe which he carried out together with his assistants and pupils, many of whom were independent masters. Painted religious, mythological, allegorical, and historical subjects, hunting and battle scenes, landscapes, and portraits.

44. *The Adoration of the Shepherds*
Oil on canvas (transferred from wood in 1868),
25 × 18½ in. (63.5 × 47 cm.)
Inv. no. 492

This sketch is a model for the altarpiece *The Adoration of the Shepherds*, which once hung in the Constantine chapel in the Oratorian Church of Santo Spirito (San Filippo Neri) in the Italian town of Fermo. (The altarpiece is now in the Pinacoteca Comunale, Fermo.) Documents from the archive of the archbishop of Fermo, published by Jaffé (1963), show that in February 1608 Rubens was commissioned by Flaminio Ricci, rector of the Oratorians in Rome, to paint a Nativity for the church in Fermo. This was Rubens's second major commission in Italy, and together with his altarpiece for Santa Maria in Vallicella, Rome, represents the culmination of his Italian period. These two commissions established him as one of the leading painters in Rome, and in a letter of March 12, 1608, accompanying Rubens's receipt of twenty-five scudi in payment for "a painting depicting the Nativity," Ricci wrote: "I did not wish to specify the composition or other particulars regarding the painting's figures and qualities, because my opinion of the artist was such that it would be better to leave everything to his discretion, since he is now poised on the threshold of great fame." Rubens carried out this commission with extraordinary speed, and on May 17, 1608, Ricci wrote to Fermo that the canvas was already far advanced. Then, less than a month later, on July 7, he reported: "The painting is finished." The present sketch would thus appear to have been painted not later than the beginning of May 1608.

The Adoration of the Shepherds has its scriptural source in Luke 2:15–21. Rubens's prototype for his treatment of this event is known to have been Correggio's *Nativity Night* ("*La Notte*") (Gemäldegalerie, Dresden), which he may have seen in the Church of San Prospero, Reggio. There are similarities both in the overall structure of the composition and in a number of details. Rubens may well have had Correggio's painting in mind when, in concluding

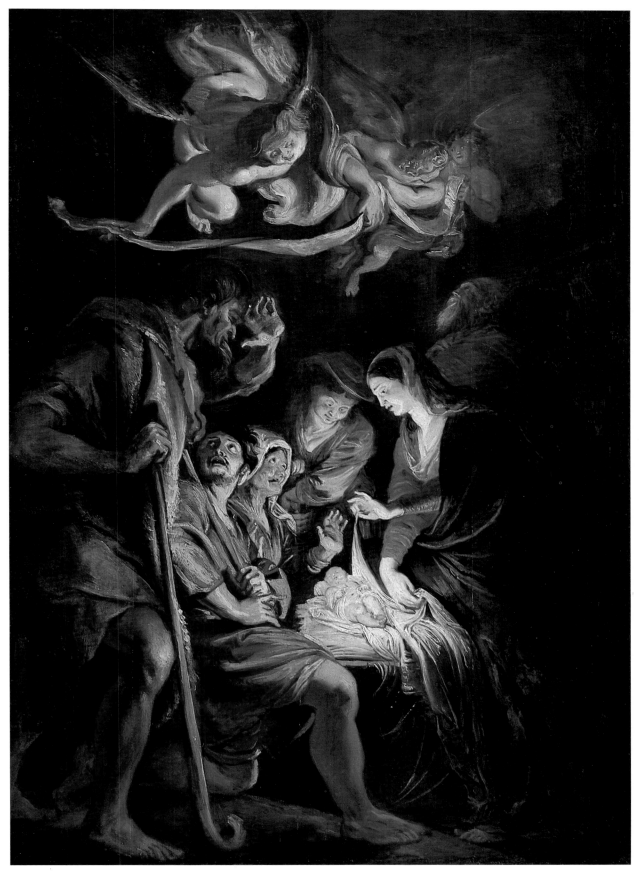

44

his contract, he promised Ricci "to paint no fewer than five large figures, namely the Madonna, Saint Joseph, three shepherds, and the baby Jesus in the manger, and furthermore to paint above the manger what is usually called a glory of angels." The deliberately homely shepherds in Rubens's sketch, who differ sharply from Correggio's idealized figures, show the influence of the great reformer of Italian painting, Caravaggio. The old woman in particular, with her hands raised in prayer and her face turned toward Mary in veneration, is a reworking of a similar figure from Caravaggio's *Madonna di Loreto* (Sant'Agostino, Rome). Further evidence of Caravaggio's impact is the strong contrast of light and shade in this sketch.

Although using Correggio's composition as his starting point, Rubens modified it to suit his own purposes. In Correggio's painting the infant is illumined by a bright light that imbues the scene with a sense of immateriality; the event seems to be a miraculous vision, a mirage. Rubens, by contrast, emphasized the palpable corporeality of each figure, inspiring belief in the reality of the scene being depicted.

A preparatory drawing for the sketch is in the Museum Fodor, Amsterdam. A copy of the altarpiece itself, executed in Rubens's studio, is in the Church of Saint Paul, Antwerp.

PROVENANCE: Acquired by the Hermitage in 1769 from the Brühl collection, Dresden
HERMITAGE CATALOGUES: 1774, no. 134; 1863–1916, no. 659; 1958, II, p. 79; 1981, p. 60
EXHIBITIONS: 1965 Brussels, no. 184; 1977 Cologne, no. 20; 1978 Leningrad, no. 17
LITERATURE: Benois [1910], p. 242; Burchard 1926–27, p. 3; Longhi 1927, pp. 191–97; Puyvelde 1952, pp. 101, 201, note 33; Held 1959, I, p. 101; Gerson and Kuile 1960, pp. 76–77, 184, note 30; Jaffé 1963, pp. 232–34, 240; Varchavskaya 1975, pp. 55–60; Vsevolozhskaya and Linnik 1975, pls. 155–57; Held 1980, pp. 446–47, no. 321

NG

Detail: Plate 44 ▷

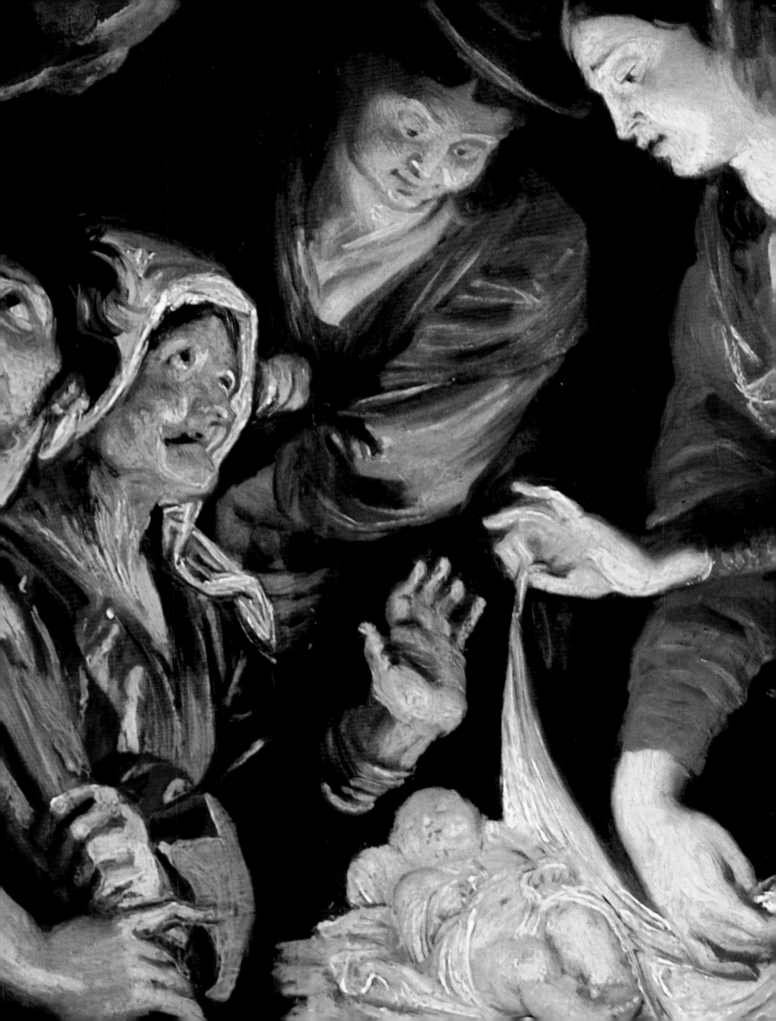

PETER PAUL RUBENS

45. *Roman Charity*

Oil on canvas (transferred from wood in 1846),
55⅜ × 71 in. (140.5 × 180.3 cm.)
Inv. no. 470

In *Factorum et dictorum memorabilium libri ix* (5:4) Valerius Maximus recounts a story that became emblematic of filial piety. Pero, a young Roman woman, saved her father, Cimon, who had been sentenced to death by starvation, by suckling him at her breast. Rubens painted several versions of this scene, of which this painting is the earliest. Its composition corresponds to Pompeian frescoes that depict the same subject, but several scholars have suggested that Rubens might also have been familiar with other, now lost antique depictions of Cimon and Pero. With its clarity of compositional structure and its plastic figural modeling, the Hermitage painting is one of the finest examples of Rubens's "classical" period. But if the beauty of the figures demonstrates the lessons Rubens learned in studying antique art and particularly the antique canon of proportions, the beauty of the painting itself clearly points to the Netherlandish love of saturated, "open" colors. On first impression the painting seems rather cold, because of the precise rationalism of its construction, the serene and balanced composition, and the restricted palette, all of which Rubens adopted from Renaissance art. However, the painting has a great deal of inner emotion. The strong spiritual bond that unites father and daughter is expressed through the static, classical form of the pyramid, which underscores the drama of the scene.

This work is stylistically similar to Rubens's *Jupiter and Callisto* (Gemäldegalerie, Kassel), signed and dated 1613. In the Kassel work, however, the relationship between the figures is somewhat more complex and a landscape has been added; the picture also shows the brownish palette associated with Rubens's first post-Italian works. These differences suggest a date of about 1612 for the Hermitage painting.

The composition was partially adopted by Artus Quellinus (1609–1668), a sculptor from Rubens's circle, in two works: the general figural placement can be seen in his terracotta *Samson and Delilah* (Staatliche Museen, Berlin-Dahlem), while the head of Pero appears in the terracotta model of *Cimon and Pero*, a sculpture intended for an uncompleted fountain in the courtyard of the Amsterdam town hall (Rijksmuseum, Amsterdam).

The Hermitage painting or a copy of it was engraved in the late seventeenth century by Cornelis van Ceucercken (Voorhelm-Schneevoogt 1873, p. 141, no. 48).

PROVENANCE: Acquired by the Hermitage in 1768 from the Cobentzl collection, Brussels; in the late seventeenth century was possibly in the collection of Carl van den Bosch, Bishop of Brussels
HERMITAGE CATALOGUES: 1774, no. 30; 1863–1916, no. 1785; 1958, II, p. 79; 1981, p. 61
EXHIBITIONS: 1978 Leningrad, no. 21; 1985 Rotterdam, no. 36

LITERATURE: Livret 1838, p. 363, no. 13; Smith 1839, II, p. 159, no. 556; Smith 1842, IX, p. 303, no. 218; Waagen 1864, p. 138; Rooses 1890, IV, pp. 105–7, no. 870; Neustroyev 1909, p. 23; Benois [1910], p. 224; Shmidt 1926, p. 16; Varchavskaya 1975, pp. 72–75, no. 5; Varchavskaya 1981, pp. 8–9

NG

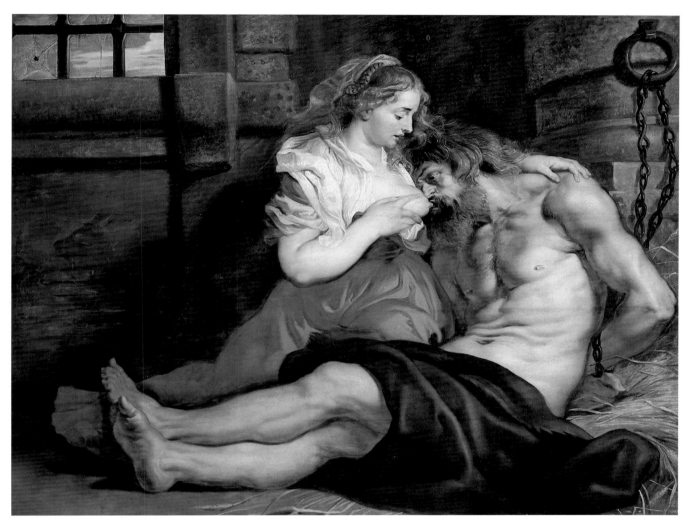

45

PETER PAUL RUBENS

46. *Landscape with Stone Carriers*
Oil on canvas (transferred from wood in 1823),
33⅞ × 49¾ in. (86 × 126.5 cm.)
Inv. no. 480

Although one of Rubens's favorite genres was landscape, he usually painted such works for his own pleasure. This perhaps explains the large number of landscapes listed in the inventory of his collection that was made after his death. Rubens's interest in this genre was evident during his years in Italy, but it was not until the end of the 1620s, when he was in his forties, that he produced his first landscapes. He always treats the landscape as a grandiose universalized panorama rather than as a modest corner of some actual locality. His landscapes are imbued with heroic, cosmic elements. The stormy dynamism of his figure paintings in the years around 1620 is especially evident in the early group of landscapes to which the Hermitage canvas, painted about 1620, belongs. This work is of particular interest because in it Rubens pays tribute to an artist he respected highly, the German painter Adam Elsheimer (1578–1610), of whom he wrote enthusiastically that as a landscapist "he had no equal." Here the evening landscape on the left, with the moon and its watery reflection, is heavily indebted to Elsheimer's *Flight into Egypt* (Alte Pinakothek, Munich). Rubens knew the work well and advised the painter's widow to send it to Flanders, "where the painter has so many admirers."

The cart is taken from Rubens's drawing *Farmyard with Farmer and Cart* of about 1615–17 (formerly in the Devonshire collection, Chatsworth; Christie's, London, July 3, 1984, lot no. 52). The painting also incorporates, with minor alterations, elements from another drawing by Rubens, *The Dry Willow* (ca. 1620; British Museum, London).

The painting has been frequently copied and engraved. In the seventeenth century both Boetius and Schelte Adams Bolswert made engravings of it (Voorhelm-Schneevoogt 1873, p. 233, no. 53:5), as did several anonymous engravers.

PROVENANCE: Acquired by the Hermitage in 1779 from the Walpole collection, Houghton Hall, England; in 1661 possibly in the Mazarini collection, Paris; subsequently in the Potter collection, The Hague, and the Cadogan collection, London
HERMITAGE CATALOGUES: 1863–1916, no. 594; 1958, II, p. 82; 1981, p. 62
EXHIBITIONS: 1967 Montreal, no. 80; 1972 Warsaw, no. 84; 1975–76 Washington, D.C., no. 16; 1977 Antwerp, no. 42; 1978 Leningrad, no. 32; 1981 Vienna, pp. 112–15; 1985 Sapporo, no. 27
LITERATURE: Aedes Walpolianae 1752, p. 87, no. 44; Smith 1830, II, p. 157, no. 547; Livret 1838, p. 12, no. 24; Waagen 1864, p. 143; Rooses 1890, IV, pp. 369–70, no. 1178; Shmidt 1926, p. 23; Glück 1945, pp. 18, 56, no. 7; Grossmann 1951, p. 20, no. 65; Held 1959, I, pp. 34, 144, 146; Varchavskaya 1975, pp. 127–31, no. 19; Vergara 1982, pp. 48–55

NG

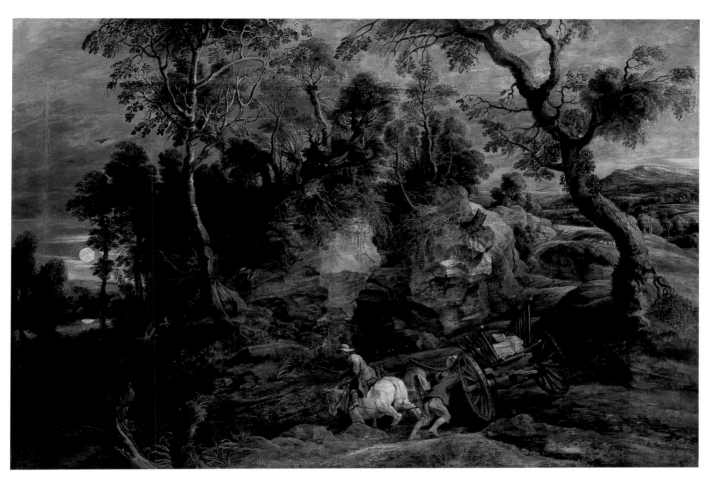

46

PETER PAUL RUBENS

47. *The Arch of Ferdinand*
   Oil on canvas (transferred from wood in 1864),
     41 × 28½ in. (104 × 72.5 cm.)
   Inv. no. 502

This is a sketch for the decoration of Antwerp on the occasion of the triumphal entry, on April 17, 1635, of the new governor-general of the Netherlands, Cardinal-Infante Ferdinand, successor to Archduchess Isabella and brother of the Spanish king Philip IV. In November 1634 the Antwerp town council commissioned Rubens to design temporary wooden structures decorated with painting and sculpture. Under his supervision and using his plans, a large group of Antwerp artists created a remarkable decorative ensemble. Today the only surviving records of the project are Rubens's sketches (most of them in the Hermitage) and engravings by his pupil Theodor van Thulden (1606–1669), which were published in 1642, after Rubens's death, in a book commemorating Ferdinand's visit.

   In developing a program for the city decorations, Rubens collaborated with two prominent Antwerp humanists: Nicolaes Rockox, a scholar, collector, and former burgomaster, and Jan Caspar Gevartius (Govarts), who was secretary of the town council and a writer and authority on classical authors.

   This sketch shows the reverse side of the arch that stood at the entrance to New Street. The arch celebrated Ferdinand's victory over the Swedish army, which he achieved with his ally, the Hungarian king Ferdinand (the future Emperor Ferdinand III), outside Nördlingen, Bavaria, on September 4–5, 1634.

   The main scene above the arch's central bay is *The Triumph of Ferdinand After the Battle of Nördlingen.* Ferdinand rides in his chariot, while a Victory crowns him; a second Victory, accompanied by Hope, flies above him holding a trophy and a palm branch, symbol of peace. In front of the chariot are a bust representing the genius of the city of Nördlingen and an imperial standard (*labarum*) with the letter *F.* Captives are grouped to either side of the chariot, while a standard-bearer and a soldier who carries a trophy occupy the foreground. The coat of arms of the Spanish king, guarded by lions, is shown above the painting with the inscription AUSPICE PHILIPPI MAGNI REGIS (under the aegis of King Philip the Great). The picture is flanked by statues: to the left Honor holds a scepter and cornucopia; to the right Valor, clothed in a lion skin, holds a club and sword. In the left niche the king's generosity is personified by a figure scattering coins from a cornucopia; the inscription below reads LIBERALIT. REGI. In the right niche Foresight holds a globe and helm; the inscription below reads PROVIDENT. The medallion above the left bay shows Nobility with the inscription NOBILIT. Above the right bay Ferdinand as a youth is depicted; the inscription in the medallion's background reads JUVENT., and that below it JUVENTAS FERD. P. Trumpeters, trophies, shackled captives, and Victories with shields appear on left and right. On the shield of the Victory at the right is inscribed FIDES MILITUM (loyalty to the army). On the cornice at the left, beneath a group of captives, is the inscription HAUD VIRES AC[QUIRIT EUNDO] (His fame cannot grow any greater), a paraphrase of a verse from Virgil's *Aeneid* (4:174): VIRESQUE ACQUIRIT EUNDO (His fame grows greater and greater). The arch is crowned by a winged horse and the scarcely discernible figure of the Morning Star (Lucifer) or Aurora.

The Arch of Ferdinand was apparently the first of Rubens's sketches for the Antwerp decorations. Martin (1972) has published documents that allow the sketch to be dated to before November 24, 1634, when the wooden skeleton of the arch was commissioned.

The composition was engraved by Theodor van Thulden in *Pompa introitus . . . Ferdinandi . . .* (1642; pls. 28, 29).

PROVENANCE: Acquired by the Hermitage in 1779 from the Walpole collection, Houghton Hall, England; was earlier in the collection of Prosper Hendrik Lankrink, London
HERMITAGE CATALOGUES: 1863–1916, no. 564; 1958, II, p. 94; 1981, p. 64
EXHIBITIONS: 1968 Göteborg, pp. 28–30; 1977 Antwerp, no. 95; 1978 Leningrad, no. 48; 1979–80 Melbourne–Sydney, no. 31

LITERATURE: Aedes Walpolianae 1752, p. 70; Waagen 1864, pp. 145–46; Rooses 1890, III, pp. 310–13, no. 783; Neustroyev 1909, p. 64; Benois [1910], p. 230; Shmidt 1926, p. 181; Puyvelde 1939, p. 43; Evers 1943, pp. 188–89; Roeder-Baumbach and Evers 1943, pp. 65–66, 106, 152; Varchavskaya 1967, pp. 283, 289; Martin 1972, pp. 156–58; Varchavskaya 1975, pp. 213–16, no. 37; Held 1980, pp. 236–38

NG

PETER PAUL RUBENS

48. *The Arch of Hercules*
Oil on canvas (transferred from wood in 1871),
40½ × 28⅜ in. (103 × 72 cm.)
Inv. no. 503

This is one of Rubens's sketches for the decoration of Antwerp on the occasion of the entry, on April 17, 1635, of Cardinal-Infante Ferdinand (see cat. no. 47). It shows the front of the arch erected on Monastery Street, at the entrance to the cloister of Saint Michael, the governor-general's residence.

Above the central bay of the arch is a depiction of Hercules at the Crossroads. Vice is represented by Venus, who stands with Bacchus and Cupid, and Virtue by Minerva, who summons the hero to the temple of fame.

Ferdinand's military victories had begun to open a path to peace and prosperity for the Spanish Netherlands, and this welcome aspect of the governor-general's services was glorified in the completed decorative cycle. The Arch of Hercules and the Arch of Ferdinand contain no military attributes, except for two flaming bombshells which are not so much attributes of war as emblems of the sovereign's "military prudence" (Held 1980). The present arch is crowned by a palm tree, a symbol of virtue, justice, and moral victory; the palm is winged to signify victory, fame, peace, and reason and is flanked by banners and by

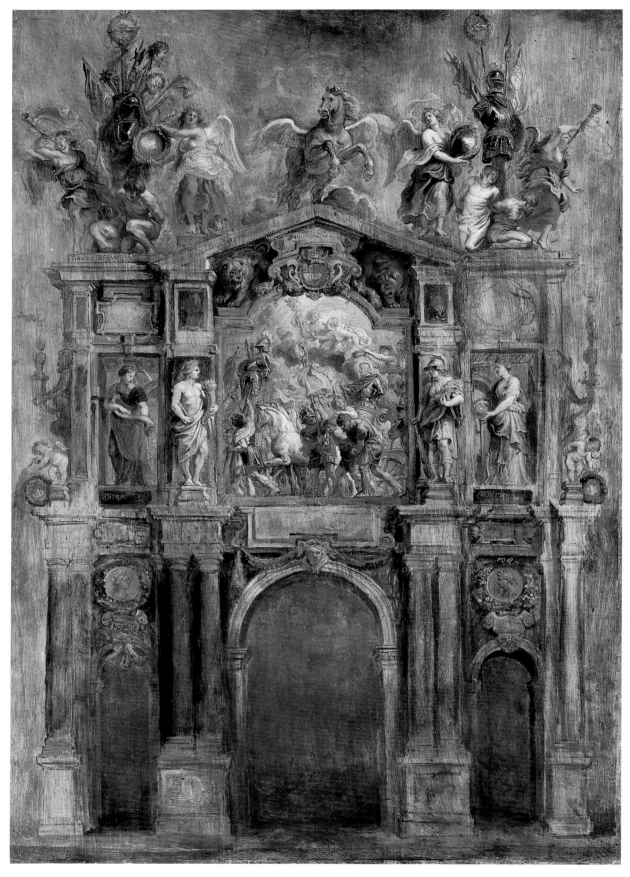

47

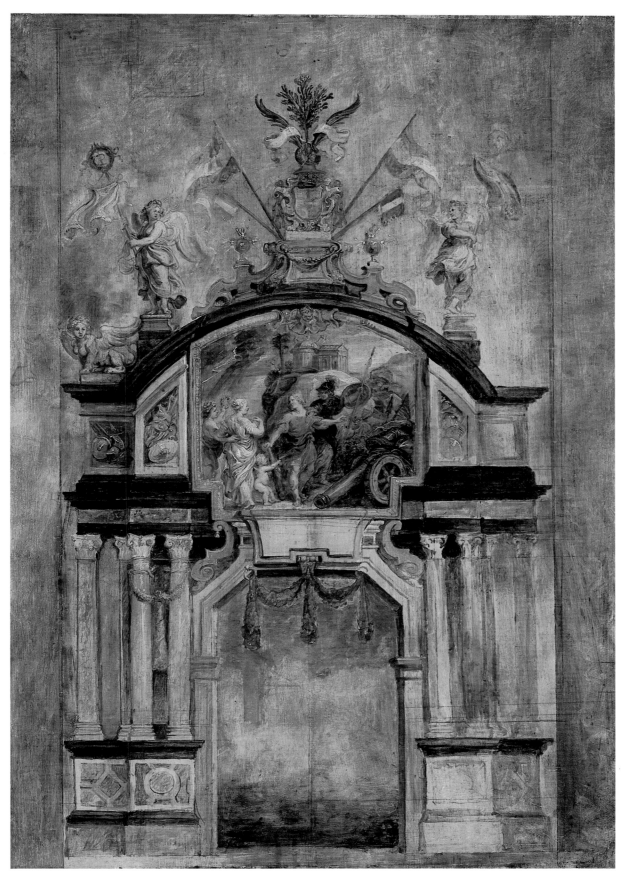

48

two Victories holding the military standards of Philip and Ferdinand. In the cartouche is found a sphinx, symbol of sobriety, courage, and good sense.

Martin (1972) has published documents that allow the sketch to be dated after January 5, 1635, when the Fugger banking house provided the city with additional funds for the construction of a third arch in addition to those of Philip and Ferdinand.

The composition was engraved by Theodor van Thulden in *Pompa introitus . . . Ferdinandi . . .* (1642; pls. 37, 38).

PROVENANCE: Acquired by the Hermitage in 1779 from the Walpole collection, Houghton Hall, England; was earlier in the collection of Prosper Hendrik Lankrink, London

HERMITAGE CATALOGUES: 1863–1916, no. 563; 1958, II, p. 94; 1981, p. 65

EXHIBITIONS: 1968–69 Belgrade, no. 20; 1977 Antwerp, no. 96; 1978 Leningrad, no. 51

LITERATURE: Aedes Walpolianae 1752, p. 70; Waagen 1864, pp. 145–46; Rooses 1890, III, p. 322–23, no. 788; Neustroyev 1909, p. 66; Benois [1910], p. 229; Shmidt 1926, pp. 20–22; Panofsky 1930, p. 121; Roeder-Baumbach and Evers 1943, pp. 68–69, 106, 174; Puyvelde 1952, p. 159; Varchavskaya 1967, pp. 283–85, 286; Martin 1972, pp. 208–9; Varchavskaya 1975, pp. 225–28, no. 40; Held 1980, pp. 245–46, no. 165

NG

Detail: Plate 47 ▷

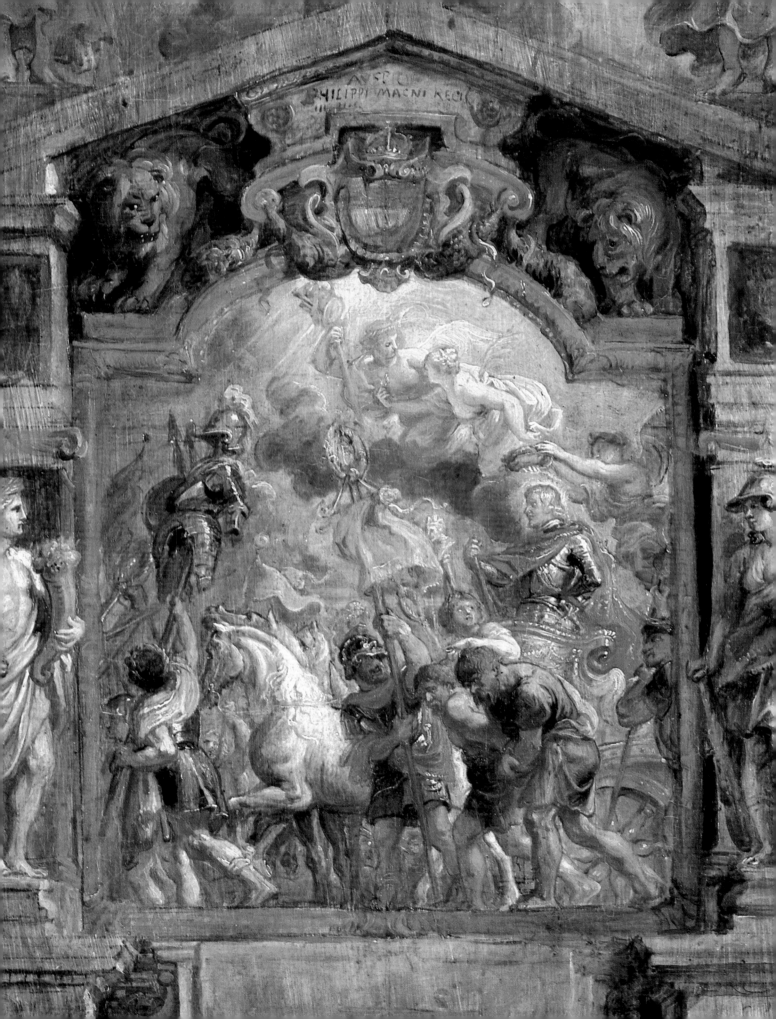

FRANS SNYDERS

1579 Antwerp–1657 Antwerp
Studied with Pieter Brueghel the Younger and possibly also with Hendrik van
Balen. Master of the Antwerp Guild of Saint Luke (1602). Worked in Italy
(1608–9). On return to Antwerp became a close friend of Rubens and
often collaborated with him, as well as artists in his circle, among them
Anthony van Dyck, Jacob Jordaens, Cornelis de Vos, and Jan Boeckhorst.
Painted still lifes and animals.

49. *Fruit in a Bowl on a Red Cloth*
    Oil on canvas (transferred from wood in 1867),
       23½ × 35¾ in. (59.8 × 90.8 cm.)
    Inv. no. 612

The still life was one of the most innovative forms in seventeenth-century
Flemish art. It proved to be a particularly direct medium for manifesting the
life-affirming spirit that Rubens had introduced. The flowers, fruits, vegetables,
fish, and game depicted in Flemish still lifes have such abundant energy and
strength—they radiate such an exultant joy in earthly existence—that it is
impossible to apply the term *nature morte* to them. These vital qualities are
present in Snyders's work, most strikingly in his large monumental "Shops,"
but no less so in his dynamic and heroically conceived cabinet pieces, of which
the Hermitage's *Fruit in a Bowl on a Red Cloth* is an example.

    The central motif—a large faience bowl filled with fruit—is typical of
Snyders's earliest still lifes. The painting can be dated to about 1616 because of
its similarity to a group of works by Snyders painted between 1610 and 1616.
In its composition and execution it most closely resembles his *Basket of Grapes
with a Parrot and Cat*, dated 1616 (formerly in a private collection, London;
reproduced in Robels 1969, ill. 36). A second version of the painting, *Fruit in a
Bowl and Shells on a Table*, is in the Gemäldegalerie, Berlin-Dahlem.

PROVENANCE: Acquired by the Hermitage
before 1797
HERMITAGE CATALOGUES: 1863–1916, no.
1318; 1958, II, p. 100; 1981, p. 69
EXHIBITIONS: 1977 Tokyo–Kyoto, no. 13;
1978 Leningrad, no. 77; 1985 Rotterdam,
no. 38
LITERATURE: Livret 1838, p. 220, no. 77;
Waagen 1864, p. 269; Benois [1910], p. 239;
Levinson-Lessing 1926, p. 19

NG

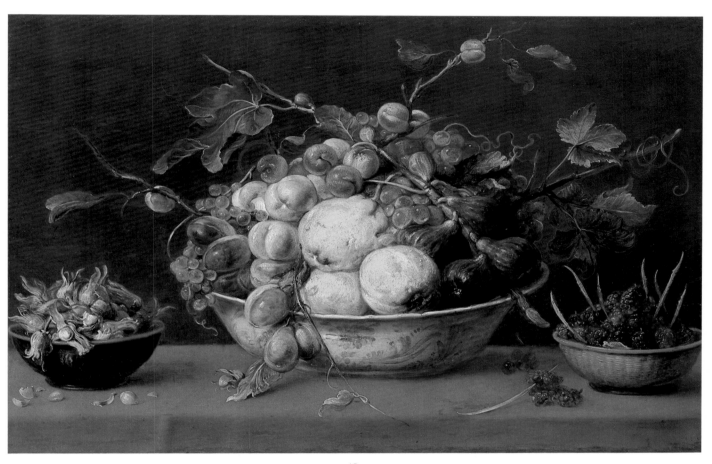

49

MICHAEL SWEERTS

1618 Brussels–1664 Goa
Lived in Rome (1646–52/54?). Mentioned in Brussels (1656), where
the town council allowed him to establish a drawing academy, which was
short-lived. Joined a religious community, the Société des Missions Etrangères
(1660). Accompanied Bishop François Pallu to Marseilles (1661) and then on
a voyage to the East. Quarreled with his traveling companions and moved
from Isfahan to Goa, the center for Portuguese Jesuits, where he died in
1664. Painted portraits, genre scenes, and religious and allegorical subjects.

50. *Portrait of a Young Man (Self-portrait)*
Oil on canvas, 44⅞ × 36¼ in. (114 × 92 cm.)
Signed and dated on paper attached to tablecloth: A.D. 1656
Ratio Quique Reddenda Michael/Sweerts F
Inv. no. 3654

The profound melancholy of this young man has long been singled out
as the dominant psychological feature of this portrait. In the old catalogues of
the gallery of the Academy of Arts the painting was called *The Bankrupt*,
because of the still life included in the composition. The books, the inkwell
and quills, and the purse and coins gave rise to a theory that the painting
showed a man of business in his study, in the tradition of depictions of
moneychangers or notaries so popular in Netherlandish painting. It was there-
fore assumed that the sitter's mood was connected to his financial difficulties.
Neustroyev (1907) cast doubt on this interpretation. Valentiner (1930) and a
number of other, later authors (among them, Hall 1963 and Raupp 1984)
proposed that the painting is a self-portrait of Sweerts. A comparative analysis
and certain iconographic peculiarities in the portrait argue in favor of this
opinion. The figure in the Hermitage canvas is similar to that in a self-portrait
by Sweerts in the Manuel Gasser collection, Zurich. Raupp has shown that the
painting is a *pensieroso* (pensive) portrait, based on the fifteenth-century
Neoplatonic concept that melancholy is the distinguishing feature of the creative
character. Dürer's famous engraving *Melencolia I* (1514) established a paradigm
that prevailed for several centuries. The characteristic pose of the head resting
on the hand found in Dürer's print is repeated here and is found in a great
many self-portraits by seventeenth-century Dutch masters.

The allegorical significance of the objects in the painting is consistent
with this interpretation. The old books, empty purse, gold coins, and inkwell
are all typical symbols of *vanitas* and are seen in many Dutch still lifes that express the transitoriness of earthly existence. The Hermitage portrait is further
elucidated by its moralizing inscription, RATIO QUIQUE REDDENDA (Every man
must give an accounting). This allegorical strain is characteristic of Sweerts's art.

PROVENANCE: Transferred to the Hermitage
in 1922 from the Museum of the Academy
of Arts, Petrograd; in the I. I. Shuvalov
collection in Saint Petersburg until 1863
HERMITAGE CATALOGUES: 1958, II, p. 268
(Dutch school); 1981, p. 68 (Flemish school,
seventeenth–eighteenth centuries)
EXHIBITIONS: 1938 Leningrad, no. 173; 1972

Moscow, p. 70; 1985 Rotterdam, no. 40
LITERATURE: Ukazatel 1842, no. 657; Somov
1874, no. 537; Martin 1907, pp. 133–56;
Neustroyev 1907, p. 38; Valentiner 1930,
no. 1; Plietzsch 1960, p. 211; Hall 1963,
no. 2045:2; Bloch 1965, pp. 168, 169, 171;
Bloch 1968, p. 23, pl. 19; Kuznetsov and
Linnik 1982, pls. 44, 45; Raupp 1984, p. 230

IS

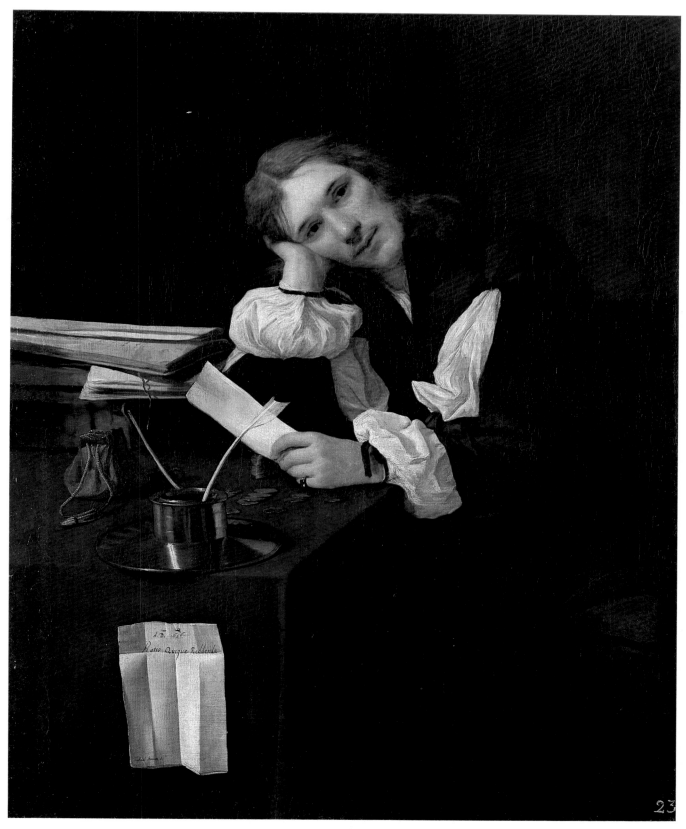

DAVID TENIERS II

1610 Antwerp–1690 Brussels
Son and pupil of David Teniers the Elder. Joined the Antwerp painters' guild
(1632). Moved to Brussels (1651), where he became court painter to the
Spanish governor-general, Archduke Leopold Wilhelm, and keeper of his art
gallery. Actively involved in organizing the Antwerp Academy of Arts
(mid-1660s). Painted genre scenes, landscapes, animals, depictions of picture
galleries, portraits, and still lifes, as well as religious, mythological, and
allegorical subjects.

51. *Monkeys in a Kitchen*
Oil on canvas (transferred from wood), 14⅛ × 19¾ in.
(36 × 50 cm.)
Signed lower right: D. TENIERS.F.
Inv. no. 568

The iconography and composition of Teniers's painting in the Hermitage is
taken from Frans Francken II's *The Monkeys' Kitchen* (Wilhelm-Lembruck-
Museum, Duisburg).

Teniers has endowed these animals with grotesquely satirical features, in
contrast to his more naturalistic animal sketches (cf. *Studies of Monkey Heads*,
Musées Royaux d'Art et d'Histoire, Brussels). The motif of monkeys imitating
human activities—for example, playing cards as in the Hermitage painting
—recurs in many of Teniers's works, where he uses it to embody such themes
as the senseless copying of nature (*The Monkey Artist*) and the soulless approach to classical art (*The Monkey Sculptor*; both in the Prado, Madrid).

In the Hermitage painting the monkeys are all differentiated according to
their costumes and their positions (the leader of the group, for instance, occupies the stool, in a parody of the social order in human society).

Teniers's series of Monkeys was used in political satire in the late eighteenth century. During the Directorate, one of these paintings was copied in a
French broadsheet under the title *The Majority and Minority in the Directorate*.
However, Teniers's signature was not reproduced in full by the anonymous
engraver, who also added a different date: "Tenier px. 1797" (Musée Carnavalet
1977, p. 42, no. 210; the catalogue also mentions a similar etching—*Five
Monkeys*—without naming Teniers and his painting as the source).

Rosenberg (1901) dates the Hermitage canvas to the middle of Teniers's
career (1640–60), Smolskaya (1962) to the mid-1640s. There is a version in the
Dullière collection, Brussels (oil on wood, 12⅝ × 18⅞ in. [32 × 48 cm.]), and
two analogous works by Teniers, both called *Feasting Monkeys*, are in the Alte
Pinakothek, Munich, and the Prado, Madrid.

PROVENANCE: Acquired by the Hermitage
in 1815 from the collection of Empress
Josephine at Malmaison; was earlier in the
collection of the Landgrave of Hesse, Kassel
HERMITAGE CATALOGUES: 1863–1916,
no. 699; 1958, p. 108; 1981, p. 75
EXHIBITIONS: 1960b Leningrad, p. 8; 1983
Tokyo, no. 16; 1985 Rotterdam, pp. 128,
137, no. 41
LITERATURE: Livret 1838, p. 398; Somov
1859, p. 110; Waagen 1864, p. 162;
Neustroyev 1898, p. 233; Rosenberg 1901,
p. 93; Rooses 1902, pp. 120, 122;
Wurzbach 1910, II, p. 698; Bode 1958,
p. 539; Wilenski 1960, I, p. 667; Smolskaya
1962, pp. 13, 14; Grandjean 1964, p. 151,
no. 1073; Levinson-Lessing 1964, no. 23;
Bénézit 1976, X, p. 113; Linnik and
Piotrovsky 1984, no. 68

NB

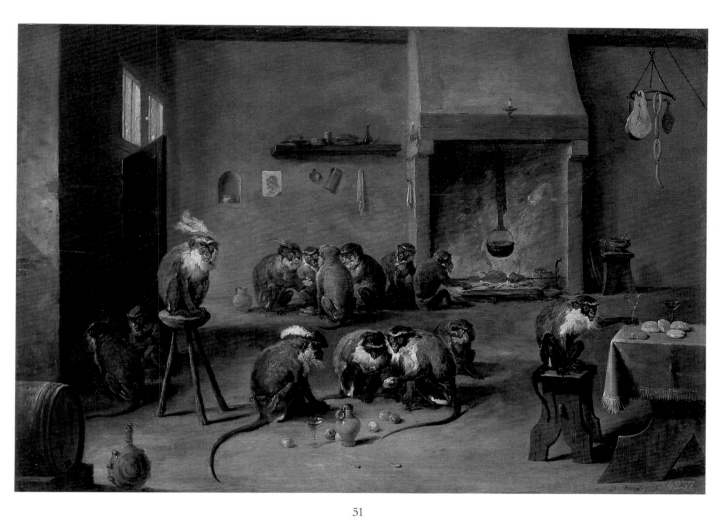

51

EXHIBITIONS

BIBLIOGRAPHY

EXHIBITIONS

1908 Saint Petersburg
Starye gody [Bygone days]. Saint Petersburg, Nov.–Dec. 1908

1910 Brussels
Exposition d'art ancien: Trésors de l'art belge au XVIIe siècle. Brussels, Nouveau Palais, 1910

1915 Petrograd
Pamiati P. P. Semenova-Tian-Shanskogo: Vystavka [In memory of P. P. Semenov-Tianshansky: An exhibition]. Petrograd, 1915

1936 Moscow–Leningrad
Rembrandt van Rijn. Moscow–Leningrad, 1936

1938 Leningrad
Vystavka portreta, vyp. 3: Portret epokhi vosrozhdeniia i barokko [Exhibition of portraits, part 3: Portraits of the Renaissance and Baroque periods]. Leningrad, The State Hermitage, 1938

1956 Moscow–Leningrad
Vystavka proizvedenii Rembrandta i ego shkoly v sviazi s 350-letiem so dnia rozhdeniia [Exhibition of works by Rembrandt and his school on the occasion of the 350th anniversary of his birth]. Moscow–Leningrad, 1956

1956 Amsterdam–Rotterdam
Rembrandt, tentoonstelling ter herdenking van de geboorte van Rembrandt: Schilderijen. Amsterdam, Rijksmuseum, May 18–Aug. 5, 1956; Rotterdam, Museum Boymans, Aug. 8–Oct. 21, 1956

1960a Leningrad
Adrian fan Ostade: Vystavka proizvedenii khudozhnika k 350-letiiu so dnia rozhdeniia [Adriaen van Ostade: An exhibition of the artist's work on the occasion of the 350th anniversary of his birth]. Leningrad, 1960

1960b Leningrad
Tenirs v sobranii Ermitazha [Teniers in the Hermitage collection]. Leningrad, 1960

1965 Brussels
Le siècle de Rubens. Brussels, Musées Royaux des Beaux-Arts de Belgique, Oct. 15–Dec. 12, 1965

1967 Montreal
Terre des hommes: Exposition internationale des beaux-arts. Montreal, Expo 1967, Apr. 28–Oct. 27, 1967

1968 Tokyo–Kyoto
Masterpieces of Rembrandt. Tokyo National Museum, Apr. 2–May 16, 1968; Kyoto National Museum, May 25–July 14, 1968

1968 Göteborg
Eremitaget Leningrad—Göteborg Konstmuseum: 100 malningar och teckningar fran Eremitaget, Leningrad, västeuropeisk konst fran 1500–1700 talen. Göteborgs Konstmuseum, 1968

1968–69 Belgrade
Stari Majstori iz Ermitazhe: Dela zapadnoevropskich slikara 16–18 veka iz zbirki dozhavnogo Ermitazha. Belgrade, Narodni Muzej u Beogradu, Nov. 1968–Jan. 1969

1969 Leningrad
Rembrandt, ego predshestvenniki i posledovateli [Rembrandt, his precursors and followers]. Leningrad, 1969

1969 Amsterdam
Rembrandt 1669–1969. Amsterdam, Rijksmuseum, Sept. 13–Nov. 30, 1969

1971 Tokyo–Kyoto
100 Masterpieces from U.S.S.R. Museums. Tokyo–Kyoto, 1971

1972 Leningrad
Iskusstvo portreta [The art of the portrait]. Leningrad, The State Hermitage, 1972

1972 Moscow
Portret v evropeiskoi zhivopisi XV–nachala XX veka [The portrait in European painting from the 15th to the early 20th century]. Moscow, 1972

1972 Dresden
Jubiläumsausstellung "250 Jahre Gemäldegalerie": Meister-werke aus der Eremitage Leningrad und aus dem Puschkin-Museum Moskau. Dresden, Albertinum, July 1–Aug. 27, 1972

1972 Warsaw
Europäische Landschaftsmalerei 1550–1650: Eine Gemein-schafts-Ausstellung des Nationalmuseums Warschau, der Nationalgalerie Prag, des Museums der Bildenden Künste Budapest, der Staatlichen Eremitage Leningrad und der Gemaldegalerie Alte Meister, Dresden. Warsaw–Prague–Leningrad–Dresden, 1972

1973 Leningrad
Karavadzho i karavadzhisty [Caravaggio and the Cara-vaggisti]. Leningrad, 1973

1974 The Hague–Münster
Gerard Ter Borch. The Hague, Mauritshuis, March 9–Apr. 28, 1974; Münster, Landesmuseum, May 12–June 23, 1974

1974 Geneva
De Genève à l'Ermitage: Les collections de François Tronchin. Geneva, Musée Rath, Nov. 12–Dec. 16, 1974

1974 Le Havre
Maîtres flamands et hollandais du Musée de l'Ermitage. Le Havre, Musée des Beaux-Arts, Nov. 12–Dec. 16, 1974

1975–76 Washington, D.C.
Master Paintings from the Hermitage and the State Russian Museum, Leningrad. Washington, D.C., National Gallery of Art; New York, M. Knoedler & Co.; The Detroit Institute of Art; Los Angeles County Museum of Art; Houston, The Museum of Fine Arts, 1975–76

1977 Antwerp
P. P. Rubens: Paintings—Oil Sketches—Drawings. Antwerp, Koninklijk Museum voor schone Kunsten, June 29–Sept. 30, 1977

1977 Cologne
Peter Paul Rubens, 1577–1640: Rubens in Italien, Gemälde, Ölskizzen, Zeichnungen. Cologne, Kunsthalle, 1977

1977 Tokyo–Kyoto
Master Paintings from the Hermitage Museum, Leningrad [in Japanese]. Tokyo, The National Museum of Western Art, Sept. 10–Oct. 23, 1977; The Kyoto Municipal Museum of Art, Nov. 4–Dec. 11, 1977

1978 Leningrad
Rubens i flamandskoe barokko: Vystavka k 400-letiiu so dnia rozhdeniia Pitera Paulia Rubensa, 1577–1640 [Rubens and the Flemish Baroque: An exhibition to commemo-rate the 400th anniversary of the birth of Peter Paul Rubens, 1577–1640]. Leningrad, 1978

1978 Prague
Padesat mistrovskych del ze sbuck sovetskych Muzee a Galerii. Prague, Narodni Galerie, 1978

1979 Leningrad
Iakob Iordans (1593–1678), zhivopis, risunok: Katalog vystavki k 300-letiiu so dnia smerti Ia. Iordansa [Jacob Jordaens (1593–1678), paintings, drawings: Exhibition catalogue to commemorate the 300th anniversary of Jacob Jordaens's death]. Leningrad, 1979

1979–80 Melbourne–Sydney
U.S.S.R., Old Master Paintings: Western European Paint-ings from the State Hermitage, Leningrad, and the A. S. Pushkin State Museum, Moscow. Melbourne, National Gallery of Victoria, Oct. 17–Dec. 2, 1979; Sydney, Art Gallery of New South Wales, Dec. 12, 1979–Feb. 10, 1980

1980 Ottawa
The Young Van Dyck. Ottawa, National Gallery of Canada, 1980

1981 Madrid
Tesoros del Ermitage. Madrid, Museo del Prado, Apr.–July 1981

1981 Vienna
Gemälde aus der Eremitage und dem Puschkin-Museum: Ausstellung von Meisterwerken des 17. Jahrhunderts aus den Staatlichen Museen von Leningrad und Moskau. Vienna, Kunsthistorisches Museum, May 13–Aug. 9, 1981

1981–82 The Hague–Cambridge, Mass.
Jacob van Ruisdael. The Hague, Koninklijk Kabinet van Schilderijen, Mauritshuis, Oct. 10, 1981–Jan. 3, 1982; Cambridge, Mass., Harvard University, Fogg Art Mu-seum, Jan. 18–April 11, 1982

1982 Tokyo
Exhibition of Paintings by Rembrandt from the Hermitage Collection [in Japanese]. Tokyo, Bridgestone Museum, Sept. 11–Nov. 3, 1982

1982–83 London
Van Dyck in England. London, National Portrait Gallery, Nov. 19, 1982–March 20, 1983

1983 Tokyo
17th Century Dutch and Flemish Paintings from the Her-mitage, Leningrad [in Japanese]. Tokyo, The National Museum of Western Art, Sept. 10–Oct. 23, 1983

1983 Dresden
Das Stilleben und sein Gegenstand: Eine Gemeinschafts-ausstellung von Museen aus der UdSSR, der CSSR und der DDR. Dresden, Albertinum, Sept. 23–Nov. 30, 1983

1984 Warsaw
Arcydziela Ermitazu: Rembrandt i jego uczniowie obrazy i kyciny. Warsaw, Museum Narodowe w Warszawie, Sept. 10–Oct. 14, 1984

1984 Leningrad–Moscow
Natiurmort v evropeiskoi zhivopisi XVI–nachala XX veka: Vystavka kartin iz museev SSR i GDR [European still-life painting from the 16th to the early 20th century: Exhibition catalogue of works from museums of the U.S.S.R. and G.D.R.]. Leningrad, The State Hermitage, and Moscow, The State Pushkin Museum of Fine Arts, 1984

1985 Rotterdam
Meesterwerken uit de Hermitage Leningrad: Hollandse en Vlaamse schilderkunst van de 17e eeuw. Rotterdam, Museum Boymans-van Beuningen, May 13–July 14, 1985

1985 Sapporo
Works by Western European Masters from the Hermitage Collection [in Japanese]. Sapporo, Hokkaido-ritsu Kindai Bijutsukan, July 13–Aug. 22, 1985

BIBLIOGRAPHY

Aedes Walpolianae 1752
Aedes Walpolianae: or, a Description of the Collection of Pictures at Houghton-Hall in Norfolk, the Seat of the Right Honourable Sir Robert Walpole, Earl of Orford. 2d ed. London, 1752.

Aedes Walpolianae 1767
Aedes Walpolianae. . . . 3d ed. London, 1767.

Ahbel 1964–65
H. Ahbel. *"Hamann in Ungnade" oder "Urias und David": Zur Deutung des Gemäldes von Rembrandt in der Eremitage.* Seminar paper, Hamburg, 1964–65.

Akademiia Khudozhestv 1863
Katalog kollektsii khudozhestvennykh proizvedenii, postupivshikh po zaveshchaniiu grafa N. A. Kusheleva-Bezborodko v sobstvennost Imperatorskoi Akademii khudozhestv [Catalogue of the collection of works of art bequeathed to the Imperial Academy of Arts by Count N. A. Kushelev-Bezborodko]. Saint Petersburg, 1863.

Akademiia Khudozhestv 1868
Katalog kartinnoi galerei grafa Kusheleva-Bezborodko nyne prinadelzhashchei Imperatorskoi Akademii khudozhestv [Catalogue of the paintings gallery of Count Kushelev-Bezborodko, now belonging to the Imperial Academy of Arts]. Saint Petersburg, 1868.

Akademiia Khudozhestv 1886
Kartinnaia galereia Imperatorskoi Akademii khudozhestv, chast 3: Katalog galerei grafa N.A. Kusheleva-Bezborodko [The paintings gallery of the Imperial Academy of Arts, part 3: Catalogue of the Count Kushelev-Bezborodko Gallery]. Saint Petersburg, 1886.

Bartsch 1803–21
A. Bartsch. *Le peintre graveur.* 21 vols. Vienna, 1803–21.

Bauch 1966
K. Bauch. *Rembrandt Gemälde.* Berlin, 1966.

Baudissin 1925
K. Baudissin. "Rembrandt und Cats." *Repertorium für Kunstwissenschaft* 45 (1925), pp. 148–79.

Bazin [1958]
G. Bazin. *Musée de l'Ermitage: Les grands maîtres de la peinture.* Paris, [1958].

Beck 1972–73
H. U. Beck. *Jan van Goyen, 1596–1656.* 2 vols. Amsterdam, 1972–73.

Benesch 1935
O. Benesch. *Rembrandt: Werk und Forschung.* Vienna, 1935.

Bénézit 1976
E. Bénézit. *Dictionnaire critique et documentaire des peintres, sculpteurs, dessinateurs et graveurs.* 10 vols. Paris, 1976.

Benois [1910]
A. N. Benois, *Putevoditel po kartinnoi galeree Imperatorskogo Ermitazha* [Guide to the paintings gallery of the Imperial Hermitage]. Saint Petersburg, [1910].

Bialostocki 1957
J. Bialostocki. "Ikonographische Forschungen zu Rembrandts Werk." *Münchner Jahrbuch der bildenden Kunst* 8 (1957), p. 210.

Blanc 1857
C. Blanc. *Le trésor de la curiosité.* Paris, 1857.

Blankert 1982
A. Blankert. *Ferdinand Bol (1616–1680): Rembrandt's Pupil.* Doornspijk, 1982.

Bloch 1965
V. Bloch. "Michael Swerts und Italien." *Jahrbuch der Staatlichen Kunstsammlungen in Baden-Württemberg* 2 (1965), pp. 168–71.

Bloch 1968
———. *Michael Sweerts.* The Hague, 1968.

Bode 1873
W. von Bode. *Die Gemäldegalerie in der Kaiserlichen Eremitage: Meisterwerke der holländischen Schule.* Saint Petersburg, 1873.

Bode 1883

———. *Studien zur Geschichte der holländischen Malerei*. Brunswick, 1883.

Bode 1889

———. "Antoon van Dyck." *Die graphischen Künste* 12 (1889), pp. 39–52.

Bode 1921

———. *Die Meister der holländischen und flämischen Malerschulen*. 3d ed. Leipzig, 1921.

Bode 1956

———. *Die Meister der holländischen und flämischen Malerschulen*. 8th ed. Leipzig, 1956.

Bode 1958

———. *Die Meister der holländischen und flämischen Malerschulen*. 9th ed. Leipzig, 1958.

Bode and Binder 1914

——— and M. J. Binder. *Frans Hals: Sein Leben und seine Werke*. 2 vols. Berlin, 1914.

Bol 1973

L. J. Bol. *Die holländische Marinemalerei des 17. Jahrhunderts*. Brunswick, 1973.

Bredius 1969

A. Bredius. *Rembrandt: The Complete Edition of the Paintings*. 3d ed., rev. by H. Gerson. London, 1969.

Brière-Misme 1948

"A Dutch Intimist, Pieter Janssens Elinga," parts 1–3. *Gazette des Beaux-Arts* 31 (1947), no. 1, pp. 89–102, 151–64; 32 (1947), no. 2, pp. 159–76; 33 (1948), no. 1, pp. 347–66.

Brochhagen and Knüttel 1967

E. Brochhagen and B. Knüttel. *Holländische Malerei des 17. Jahrhunderts*. Catalogue of the Alte Pinakothek, no. 3. Munich, 1967.

Broos 1986

B. Broos et al. *De Rembrandt à Vermeer: Les peintres hollandais au Mauritshuis de La Haye* [exh. cat.: Paris, Galeries nationales du Grand Palais, Feb. 19–June 30, 1986]. The Hague, 1986.

Brown 1982

C. Brown. *Van Dyck*. Ithaca, N.Y., 1982.

Bruyn 1970

J. Bruyn. "Rembrandt and the Italian Baroque." *Simiolus* 4 (1970), pp. 28–48.

Burchard 1926–27

L. Burchard. "Skizzen des jungen Rubens." *Sitzungsberichte der kunstgeschichtlichen Gesellschaft Berlin*, Oct. 1926–May 1927.

Buschmann 1905

P. Buschmann. *Jacques Jordaens et son oeuvre*. Brussels, 1905.

Clément de Ris 1879

L. Clément de Ris. "Musées du Nord: Musée Imperial de l'Ermitage à Saint-Pétersbourg." *Gazette des Beaux-Arts* 19 (Apr. 1879), pp. 342–52.

Crozat 1755

[I. B. Lacurne de Sainte Palay.] *Catalogue des tableaux du cabinet de M. Crozat, baron de Thiers*. Paris, 1755.

Cust 1900

L. Cust. *Anthony van Dyck: An Historical Study of His Life and Works*. London, 1900.

Cuyck 1881

A. van Nicolaas Cuyck. "Rockox de Jongere, Burgemeester van Antwerpen in de XVII-de eeuw." In *Annales de l'Académie d'Archéologie de Belgique*, no. 7. Antwerp, 1881.

Delacre 1934

M. Delacre. *Recherches sur le rôle du dessin dans l'iconographie de Van Dyck: Notes complémentaires*. Mémoires de l'Académie Royale de Belgique, Classe des Beaux-Arts. Brussels, 1934.

Delbanco 1928

G. Delbanco. *Der Maler Abraham Bloemaert*. Strasbourg, 1928.

Dobrzycka 1966

A. Dobrzycka. *Jan van Goyen*. Posen, 1966.

Drost 1926

W. Drost. *Barockmalerei in den germanischen Ländern*. Potsdam, 1926.

Dumont-Wilden 1910

L. Dumont-Wilden. "Exposition de l'art belge au XVIIe siècle à Bruxelles." *Les Arts*, Oct. 1910, pp. 2–27.

Egorova 1966

K. S. Egorova. "Portrety v tvorchestve Rembrandta 1650-kh godov" [Rembrandt's portraits of the 1650s]. In *Klassicheskoe iskusstvo za rubezhom*. Moscow, 1966.

Ertz 1979

K. Ertz. *Jan Brueghel der Ältere (1568–1625): Die Gemälde, mit kritischem Oeuvrekatalog*. Cologne, 1979.

Evers 1943

H. G. Evers. *Rubens und sein Werk: Neue Forschungen*. Brussels, 1943.

Fechner 1958

E. Y. Fechner. *Iakob van Reisdal i ego kartiny v Ermitazhe* [Jacob van Ruisdael and his paintings in the Hermitage]. Leningrad, 1958.

Fechner 1963

————. *Gollandskaia peizazhnaia zhivopis XVII veka v Ermitazhe* [Dutch landscape painting of the 17th century in the Hermitage]. Leningrad, 1963.

Fechner 1971

————. "Die Bilder von Abraham Bloemaert in der Staatlichen Ermitage zu Leningrad." *Jahrbuch des kunsthistorischen Institutes der Universität Graz* 6 (1971), pp. 111–17.

Fechner 1979

————. *Gollandskaia zhanrovaia zhivopis XVII veka v sobranii Gosudarstvennogo Ermitazha* [Dutch genre painting of the seventeenth century in the collection of the State Hermitage]. Moscow, 1979.

Fechner 1981

————. *Seventeenth-Century Dutch Still Lifes in the Hermitage* [in Russian]. Moscow, 1981.

Freise 1911

K. Freise. *Pieter Lastman, sein Leben und seine Kunst: Ein Beitrag zur Geschichte der holländischen Malerei im XVII. Jahrhundert.* Leipzig, 1911.

Fromentin 1948

E. Fromentin. *The Masters of Past Time: Dutch and Flemish Painting from Van Eyck to Rembrandt.* London–New York, 1948.

Gerson 1934

H. Gerson. "The Development of Ruisdael." *The Burlington Magazine* 65 (Aug. 1934), pp. 76–80.

Gerson 1968

————. *Rembrandt Paintings.* Amsterdam, 1968.

Gerson and Kuile 1960

———— and E. H. ter Kuile. *Art and Architecture in Belgium from 1600 to 1800.* The Pelican History of Art. Harmondsworth, 1960.

Glück 1931

G. Glück. *Van Dyck, des Meisters Gemälde.* Klassiker der Kunst, 13. 2d ed. Stuttgart–Berlin, 1931.

Glück 1934

————. "Self-Portraits by Van Dyck and Jordaens." *The Burlington Magazine* 65 (Nov. 1934), pp. 194–201.

Glück 1945

————. *Die Landschaften von Peter Paul Rubens.* Vienna, 1945.

Grandjean 1964

S. Grandjean. *Inventaire après décès de l'impératrice Joséphine à Malmaison.* Preface by Pierre Schommer. Paris, 1964.

Grant 1954

M. H. Grant. *Jan van Huysum, 1682–1749: Including a Catalogue Raisonné of the Artist's Fruit and Flower Paintings.* Leigh-on-Sea, 1954.

Griesbach 1974

L. Griesbach. *Willem Kalf, 1619–1695.* Berlin, 1974.

Gritsai 1977

N. Gritsai. "Portrety Iakoba Iordansa v Ermitazhe" [Portraits by Jacob Jordaens in the Hermitage]. *TGE* 18 (1977), pp. 83–87.

Gritsai 1982

————. *Anthony van Dyck.* Leningrad, 1982.

Grossmann 1951

F. Grossmann. "Holbein, Flemish Paintings and Everhard Jabach." *The Burlington Magazine* 93 (Jan. 1951), pp. 16–25.

Gudlaugsson 1949

S. J. Gudlaugsson. "De datering van de schilderijen van Gerard Ter Borch." *Nederlandsch Kunsthistorisch Jaarboek* 2 (1949), pp. 235–67.

Gudlaugsson 1959–60

————. *Gerard ter Borch.* 2 vols. The Hague, 1959–60.

Guiffrey 1882

J. Guiffrey. *Antoine Van Dyck: Sa vie et son oeuvre.* Paris, 1882.

Haak 1968

B. Haak. *Rembrandt: Zijn leven, zijn werk, zijn tijd.* Amsterdam, 1968 (English ed.: *Rembrandt: His Life, His Work, His Time.* New York, 1969).

Hall 1963

H. van Hall. *Portretten van Nederlandse beeldende kunstenaars.* Amsterdam, 1963.

Hamann 1948

R. Hamann. *Rembrandt.* Potsdam, 1948

Heidrich 1913

E. Heidrich. *Vlämische Malerei.* Die Kunst in Bildern. Jena, 1913.

Held 1940

J. S. Held. "Jordaens' Portraits of His Family." *Art Bulletin* 22 (June 1940), pp. 70–82.

Held 1959

————, ed. *Rubens: Selected Drawings, with an Introduction and Critical Catalogue.* 2 vols. London, 1959.

Held 1961

————. "Flora, Goddess and Courtesan." In *De artibus opuscula XL: Essays in Honour of Erwin Panofsky*, pp. 201–18. New York, 1961.

Held 1969

———. *Rembrandt's "Aristotle" and Other Rembrandt Studies*. Princeton, 1969.

Held 1980

———. *The Oil Sketches of Peter Paul Rubens: A Critical Catalogue*. 2 vols. Princeton, 1980.

Held 1982

———. *Rubens and His Circle*. Princeton, 1982.

Hendrickx 1939

M. Hendrickx. "Recherches sur le portrait de Rockox par Antoine van Dyck." *Bulletin de la classe des Beaux-Arts de l'Académie Royale de Belgique* 21 (1939).

Hermitage catalogues

1774   [E. Munich.] *Catalogue des tableaux qui se trouvent dans les galeries et dans les cabinets du Palais Impérial de Saint-Pétersbourg*. Saint Petersburg, 1774.

1863–1916   *Katalog kartinnoi galerei Imperatorskogo Ermitazha* [Catalogue of the paintings gallery of the Imperial Hermitage]. Saint Petersburg–Petrograd, 1863–1916.

1958   *Gosudarstvennyi Ermitazh, otdel zapadnoevropeiskogo iskusstva: Katalog zhivopisi* [The State Hermitage, department of western European art: Catalogue of paintings], vol. 2. Leningrad–Moscow, 1958.

1981   *Gosudarstvennyi Ermitazh, zapadnoevropeiskaya zhivopis* [The State Hermitage, western European paintings]. Leningrad, 1981.

Hind 1923

A. M. Hind. *Catalogue of Drawings by Dutch and Flemish Artists Preserved in the Department of Prints and Drawings in the British Museum*. London, 1923.

Hoet 1752

G. Hoet. *Catalogus van naamlyst van schilderyen met derselven pryzen zedert een langen reeks van jaaren zoo in Holland als op andere plaatzen in het openbaar verkogt*. . . . 3 vols. in 2. The Hague, 1752. Reprint, Soest, 1976.

Hofstede de Groot 1891

C. Hofstede de Groot. "De schilder Janssens, een navolger van Pieter de Hooch." *Oud-Holland* 9 (1891), pp. 266–96.

Hofstede de Groot 1907–28

———. *Beschreibendes und kritisches Verzeichnis der Werke der hervorragendsten holländischen Maler des XVII. Jahrhunderts*. 10 vols. Esslingen–Paris, 1907–28.

Hollstein 1949–86

[F. W. H. Hollstein.] *Hollstein's Dutch and Flemish Etchings, Engravings and Woodcuts, ca. 1450–1700*. 30 vols. Amsterdam, 1949–86.

Hulst 1956

R.-A. d'Hulst. *De tekeningen van Jacob Jordaens: Bijdrage tot de geschiedenis van de XVIIe-eeuwse kunst in de zuidelijke Nederlanden*. Brussels, 1956.

Hulst 1974

———. *Jordaens Drawings*. 4 vols. Brussels–London–New York, 1974.

Hulst 1982

———. *Jakob Jordaens*. Stuttgart, 1982.

Hulst and Vey 1960

——— and H. Vey. *Van Dyck: Tekeningen en olieverfschetsen* [exh. cat.: Rotterdam, Museum Boymans-van Beuningen, July 1–Aug. 31, 1960]. Antwerp, 1960.

Jaffé 1963

M. Jaffé. "Peter Paul Rubens and the Oratorian Fathers." *Proporzioni* 4 (1963).

Jaffé 1969

———. "Reflections on the Jordaens Exhibition." *Bulletin National Gallery of Canada, Ottawa* 13 (1969).

Jantzen 1910

H. Jantzen. *Das niederländische Architekturbild*. Leipzig, 1910.

Judson 1959

R. J. Judson. *Gerrit van Honthorst: A Discussion of His Position in Dutch Art*. The Hague, 1959.

Kahr 1965

M. Kahr. "A Rembrandt Problem: Haman or Uriah?" *Journal of the Warburg and Courtauld Institutes* 28 (1965), pp. 258–73.

Kahr 1968

———. "Rembrandt's Meaning." *Oud-Holland* 83 (1968), no. 1, pp. 63–68.

Kettering 1983

A. M. Kettering. *The Dutch Arcadia: Pastoral Art and Its Audience in the Golden Age*. Montclair, N.J., 1983.

Kharinova 1923

E. Kharinova. "Gollandskie i flamandskie zhivopistsy v Pavlovskom dvortse-muzee" [Dutch and Flemish painters in the Pavlovsk Palace Museum]. *Gorod*, Jan. 1923.

Kieser 1941–42

E. Kieser. "Über Rembrandt's Verhältnis zur Antike." *Zeitschrift für Kunstgeschichte* 10, (1941–42).

Knuttel 1956
G. Knuttel. *Rembrandt: De meester en zijn werk*. Amsterdam, 1956.

Kramm 1857–64
C. Kramm. *De levens en werken der Hollandsche en Vlaamsche kunstschilders, beeldhouwers, graveurs en bouwmeesters, van den vroegsten tot op onzen tijd*. 6 vols. Amsterdam, 1857–64. Facsimile ed., Amsterdam, 1974.

Kuznetsov 1960
Y. Kuznetsov. *Adriaen van Ostade at the Hermitage* [exh. cat. in Russian]. Leningrad, 1960.

Kuznetsov 1966
————. *Zapadnoevropeiskii natiurmort* [Western European still-life painting]. Leningrad–Moscow, 1966.

Kuznetsov 1973
————. "Sur le symbolisme dans les paysages de Jacob van Ruisdael." *Bulletin du Musée National de Varsovie* 14 (1973), pp. 31–41.

Kuznetsov and Linnik 1982
———— and I. Linnik. *Dutch Painting in Soviet Museums*. New York–Leningrad, 1982.

Lacroix 1856–65
P. Lacroix. *Revue universelle des arts*. Paris–Brussels, 1856–65.

Lalive 1764
[A. L. de Lalive.] *Catalogue historique du cabinet de peinture et sculpture française de M. de Lalive*. Paris, 1764.

Larsen 1980
E. Larsen. *L'opera completa di Van Dyck*. Milan, 1980.

Le Blanc 1854–89
C. Le Blanc. *Manuel de l'amateur d'estampes*. 4 vols. Paris, 1854–89.

Levinson-Lessing 1926
V. F. Levinson-Lessing. *Sneiders i flamandskii natiurmort* [Snyders and the Flemish still life]. Leningrad, 1926.

Levinson-Lessing 1956
————. *Rembrandt van Rijn* [in Russian]. Moscow, 1956.

Levinson-Lessing 1964a
————. *The Hermitage, Leningrad: Dutch and Flemish Masters*. Introduction and notes by V. F. Levinson-Lessing and the staff of the State Hermitage. Leningrad–London, 1964.

Levinson-Lessing 1964b
————. *Gosudarstvennyi Ermitazh: Zhivopis XVII–XVIII vekov*. Vstupitelnaia statiia V. F. Levinson-Lessing [The State Hermitage: Paintings of the 17th and 18th centuries. Introductory essay by V. F. Levinson-Lessing]. Prague–Leningrad, 1964.

Levinson-Lessing 1970
————. "Sobranie kartin Fransua Tronshena: Iz istorii kollektsii Ermitazha" [The painting collection of François Tronchin in the Hermitage Museum]. *SGE* 31 (1970).

Levinson-Lessing 1971
————. *Rembrandt Harmensz van Rijn: Paintings from Soviet Museums*. Leningrad, 1971.

Liedtke 1982
W. A. Liedtke. *Architectural Painting in Delft*. Doornspijk, 1982.

Lilienfeld 1914
K. Lilienfeld. *Arent de Gelder (1645–1727): Sein Leben und seine Kunst*. The Hague, 1914.

Linnik 1956
I. Linnik. "On the Question of the Subject Matter of Rembrandt's Picture in the Hermitage" [in Russian]. *Iskusstvo*, 1956, pp. 46–50.

Linnik 1957
————. "On the Subject of Rembrandt's Picture Known as *The Fall of Haman*" [in Russian]. *SGE* 11 (1957), pp. 8–12.

Linnik 1980
————. *Dutch Paintings of the 17th Century and the Problems of Their Attribution* [in Russian]. Leningrad, 1980.

Linnik and Piotrovsky 1984
———— and B. Piotrovsky. *Western European Painting in the Hermitage*. Leningrad, 1984.

Lipgart 1912
E. F. Lipgart. "Dar grafa P. S. Stroganova Imperatorskomu Ermitazhu" [Count P. S. Stroganov's gift to the Imperial Hermitage]. *Starye gody*, Apr. 1912, pp. 33–45.

Livret 1838
[Labensky.] *Livret de la Galerie Impériale de l'Ermitage de Saint-Pétersbourg*. Saint Petersburg, 1838.

Loewenthal 1982
A. W. Loewenthal. *Joachim Wttewael and Dutch Mannerism*. Doornspijk, 1982.

Longhi 1927
R. Longhi. "*La Notte* del Rubens a Fermo." *Vita artistica* 2, no. 10 (Oct. 1927), pp. 191–97.

Louttit 1973
M. Louttit. "The Romantic Dress of Saskia van Ulenborch: Its Pastoral and Theatrical Associations." *The Burlington Magazine* 115 (1973), pp. 317–26.

Maclaren 1960
N. Maclaren. *The Dutch School, National Gallery of London*. London, 1960.

Manke 1963
I. Manke. *Emanuel de Witte, 1617–1692*. Amsterdam, 1963.

Mariette 1853–62
P. J. Mariette. *Abecedario et autres notes inédités sur les arts et les artistes. . . .* P. de Chennevières and A. de Montaiglon, eds. 2 vols. Paris, 1853–62. Reprint, Paris 1966.

Martin 1907
W. Martin. "Michiel Sweerts als schilder: Proeve van een biografie en een catalogus van zijn schilderijen." *Oud-Holland* 25 (1907), pp. 133–56.

Martin 1972
J. R. Martin. *The Decorations for the "Pompa Introitus Ferdinandi."* Corpus Rubenianum Ludwig Burchard, 16. Brussels–London–New York, 1972.

Michel 1890
E. Michel. *Jacob van Ruisdael*. Paris, 1890.

Michel 1893
———. *Rembrandt: Sa vie, son oeuvre et son temps.* Paris, 1893.

Michiels 1881
A. Michiels. *Van Dyck et ses élèves*. Paris, 1881.

Millar 1982
O. Millar. *Van Dyck in England*. London, 1982.

Moes 1897
E. W. Moes. *Iconographia Batavia: Beredeneerde lijst van geschilderte en gebeeldhouwde portretten van Noord-Nederlanders in vorige eeuwen.* 2 vols. Amsterdam, 1897.

Moes 1909
———. *Frans Hals: Sa vie et son oeuvre.* Brussels, 1909.

Moltke 1965
J. W. von Moltke. *Govaert Flinck 1615–1660*. Amsterdam, 1965.

Müller 1927
C. Müller. "Abraham Blomaert als Landschaftsmaler." *Oud-Holland* 44 (1927), pp. 193–208.

Müller 1929
———. "Studien zu Lastman und Rembrandt." *Jahrbuch der Preussischen Kunstsammlungen* 50 (1929), pp. 45–83.

Muśee Carnavalet 1977
L'Art de l'estampe et la révolution française [exh. cat.: Paris, Muśee Carnavalet, June 27–Nov. 20, 1977].

Neustroyev 1898
A. A. Neustroyev. *Kartinnaia galereia Imperatorskogo Ermitazha* [The paintings gallery of the Imperial Hermitage]. Saint Petersburg, 1898.

Neustroyev 1907
———. "Niederländische Gemälde in der Kaiserlichen Akademie der Künste zu St. Petersburg." *Zeitschrift für bildende Kunst* 18 (1907), pp. 36–40.

Neustroyev 1909
———. "Rubens i ego kartiny v galeree Imperatorskogo Ermitazha" [The paintings of Rubens at the Hermitage Museum]. *Starye gody* 1 (1909), pp. 3–23.

Nicolson 1956
B. Nicolson. "The Rijksmuseum *Incredulity* and Terbrugghen's Chronology." *The Burlington Magazine* 98 (1956), pp. 103–10.

Nicolson 1958
———. *Hendrick Terbrugghen*. London, 1958.

Nicolson 1977
———. "Stomer Brought Up-to-date." *The Burlington Magazine*, Apr. 1977, pp. 23–45.

Nicolson 1979
———. *The International Caravaggesque Movement: List of Pictures of Caravaggio and His Followers throughout Europe from 1590 to 1650.* Oxford, 1979.

Nieuwstraten 1967
J. Nieuwstraten. "Haman, Rembrandt and Michelangelo." *Oud-Holland* 82 (1967), nos. 1–2, pp. 61–63.

Panofsky 1930
E. Panofsky. *Hercules am Scheidewege und andere antike Bildstoffe in der neueren Kunst.* Leipzig–Berlin, 1930.

Pappé 1925
A. Pappé. "Bemerkungen zu einigen Neuerwerbungen der Eremitage." *Oud-Holland* 42 (1925), pp. 118–22, 153–58.

Pappé 1926
———. "Overzicht der litteratuur betreffende Nederlandsche kunst: Sowjet-Rusland." *Oud-Holland* 43 (1926), pp. 147–50, 197–200.

Pappé 1927
———. *Gollandskaia zhanrovaia zhivopis* [Dutch genre paintings]. Leningrad, 1927.

Plietzsch 1960
E. Plietzsch. *Holländische und flämische Maler des XVII. Jahrhunderts.* Leipzig, 1960.

Puyvelde 1939
L. van Puyvelde. *Die Skizzen des Peter Paul Rubens.* Frankfurt, 1939 (English ed.: *The Sketches of Rubens.* London, 1947).

Puyvelde, 1950
———. *Van Dyck.* Les peintres flamands du XVIIe siècle. Brussels–Amsterdam, 1950.

Puyvelde 1952
————. *Rubens.* Les peintres flamands du XVIIe siècle. Paris–Brussels–New York, 1952.

Puyvelde 1953
————. *Jordaens.* Les peintres flamands du XVIIe siècle. Paris–Brussels–New York, 1953.

Raupp 1984
H.-I. Raupp. *Untersuchungen zu Künstlerbildnis und Künstlerdarstellung in den Niederlanden im 17. Jahrhundert.* Hildesheim–New York, 1984.

Réau 1912
L. Réau. "La galerie de tableaux de l'Ermitage et la collection Semenov." *Gazette des Beaux-Arts* 8, ser. 4 (1912), pp. 379–96, 471–88.

Regteren Altena 1963
J. Q. van Regteren Altena. "Gabriel Metsu as a Draughtsman." *Master Drawings* 1 (1963), pp. 13–19.

Reiss 1975
S. Reiss. *Aelbert Cuyp.* London–Boston, 1975.

Rembrandt 1971
Rembrandt Garmens van Rejn: Kartiny khudozhnika v muzeiakh Sovetskogo Soiuza [Rembrandt Harmensz van Rijn: His paintings in Soviet museums]. Leningrad, 1971.

Rembrandt Corpus 1982–86
J. Bruyn et al. *A Corpus of Rembrandt Paintings.* RRP [Rembrandt Research Project]. 2 vols. The Hague–Boston–London, 1982–86.

Robinson 1974
F. W. Robinson. *Gabriël Metsu (1629–1667): A Study of His Place in Dutch Genre Paintings of the Golden Age.* New York, 1974.

Roeder-Baumbach and Evers 1943
J. Roeder-Baumbach and H. G. Evers. *Versieringen bij blijde inkomsten gebruikt in de zuidelijke Nederlanden gedurende de 16- en 17-de eeuw.* Antwerp–Utrecht, 1943.

Roh 1921
F. Roh. *Holländische Malerei.* Jena, 1921.

Romanov 1936
N. J. Romanov. "*A Landscape with Oaks* by Jan van Goyen." *Oud-Holland* 53 (1936), pp. 187–92.

Rooses 1886–92
M. Rooses. *L'oeuvre de P. P. Rubens: Histoire et description de ses tableaux et dessins.* 5 vols. Antwerp, 1886–92.

Rooses 1902
————. "Die vlämischen und niederländischen Meister in der Ermitage zu St. Petersburg." *Zeitschrift für bildende Kunst* 13 (1902), pp. 43-48, 117–22.

Rooses 1904
————. "Die Vlämischen Meister in der Ermitage: Antoon van Dyck." *Zeitschrift für bildende Kunst* 15 (1904), pp. 114–17.

Rooses 1906
————. *Jordaens' Leben und Werke.* Stuttgart–Berlin–Leipzig, 1906.

Rosenbaum 1928
A. Rosenbaum. *Der junge Van Dyck.* Munich, 1928.

Rosenberg 1901
A. Rosenberg. *Teniers der Jüngere.* Künstler Monographien, 8. 2d, rev. ed. Bielefeld–Leipzig, 1901.

Rosenberg 1928
J. Rosenberg. *Jacob van Ruisdael.* Berlin, 1928.

Rosenberg 1948
————. *Rembrandt.* 2 vols. Cambridge, Mass., 1948.

Rosenberg, Slive, and Kuile 1972
————, S. Slive, and E. H. ter Kuile. *Dutch Art and Architecture, 1600–1800.* The Pelican History of Art. Baltimore, 1972.

Schnitzler 1828
[J. H. Schnitzler.] *Notice sur les principaux tableaux du Musée Impérial de l'Ermitage à Saint-Pétersbourg.* Saint Petersburg, 1928.

Semenov 1885
P. P. Semenov. *Etiudy po istorii niderlandskoi zhivopisi na osnovanii ee obraztsov, nakhodiaschikhsia v publichnykh i chastnykh sobraniiakh Peterburga,* I [Studies in the history of Netherlandish painting based on examples in private and public Saint Petersburg collections]. Saint Petersburg, 1885.

Semenov 1906a
————. *Catalogue de la collection Semenov à Saint-Pétersbourg.* Saint Petersburg, 1906.

Semenov 1906b
————. *Etudes sur les peintres des écoles hollandaise, flamande et néerlandaise qu'on trouve dans la collection Semenov et les autres collections publiques et privées de St.-Pétersbourg.* Saint Petersburg, 1906.

Shchavinsky 1909
V. Shchavinsky. "Istoriia gollandskoi zhivopisi po kollektsii Petra Petrovicha Semenova-Tian-Shanskogo [A History of Dutch painting based on the collection of Petr Petrovich Semenov-Tianshansky]. *Starye gody* 5 (1909), pp. 229–63.

Shchavinsky 1916
————. "Kartiny gollandskikh masterovv Gatchinskom dvortse" [Paintings by Dutch masters in the Gatchina Palace]. *Starye gody,* July–Sept. 1916, pp. 68–95.

Shcherbacheva 1924
M. I. Shcherbacheva. "K novoi razveske gollandtsev v Ermitazhe" [On the new installation of Dutch paintings in the Hermitage]. *Sredi kollektsionerov* 9-12, 1924.

Shcherbacheva 1926
————. *Gollandskii natiurmort XVII* [The Dutch still life in the 17th century]. Leningrad, 1926.

Shcherbacheva 1940
————. "Kartiny Pitera Lastmana v Ermitazhe" [Paintings by Pieter Lastman in the Hermitage]. *Trudy otdela zapadnoevropeiskogo iskusstva* 1 (1940), pp. 40–41 and note 8.

Shcherbacheva 1945
————. *Natiurmort v gollandskoi zhivopisi* [Still life in Dutch painting]. Leningrad, 1945.

Shcherbacheva 1956
————. "Novye kartiny Gontgorsta v sobranii Ermitazha" [New paintings by Honthorst in the Hermitage collection]. *TGE*, no. 1 (1956), pp. 118–21.

Shcherbacheva 1964
————. "Kartiny Matiasa Stomera v Ermitazhe" [Paintings by Matthias Stomer in the Hermitage]. *SGE* 25 (1964).

Shmidt 1926
D. A. Shmidt. *Rubens and Jordaens* [in Russian]. Leningrad, 1926.

Simon 1930
K. E. Simon. *Jacob van Ruisdael: Eine Darstellung seiner Entwicklung.* Berlin, 1930.

Simon 1935a
————. "Isaack van Ruisdael" and "Jacob van Ruisdael." In U. Thieme and F. Becker, eds. *Allgemeines Lexikon der Bildenden Künstler* 29. Leipzig, 1935.

Simon 1935b
————. "Isaack van Ruisdael" and "Jacob van Ruisdael." *The Burlington Magazine* 67 (1935), pp. 7–23, 132–35.

Six 1907
J. Six. "Paul Potter." *L'Art flamand et hollandais* 7 (1907), pp. 8–12.

Slive 1965
S. Slive. *Drawings of Rembrandt.* 2 vols. New York, 1965.

Slive 1970–74
————. *Frans Hals.* Kress Foundation Studies in the History of European Art. New York, 1970–74.

Slive and Hoetink 1981
———— and H. R. Hoetink. *Jacob van Ruisdael.* New York–Amsterdam, 1981.

Smith 1829–49
J. A. Smith. *A Catalogue Raisonné of the Works of the Most Eminent Dutch, Flemish and French Painters. . . .* 9 vols. and suppl. London, 1829–49.

Smolskaya 1962
N. Smolskaya. *Teniers* [in Russian]. Leningrad, 1962.

Sokolova 1985
I. Sokolova. "Peizazhi Gerrita Berkkeide v Ermitazhe" [Landscapes by Gerrit Berckheide in the Hermitage]. *TGE* 25 (1985).

Somov 1859
A. Somov. *Kartiny Imperatorskogo Ermitazha* [Paintings in the Imperial Hermitage]. Saint Petersburg, 1859.

Somov 1874
————. *Kartinnaia galereia Imperatorskoi Akademii khudozhestv: Katalog proizvedenii zhivopisi* [The Painting Gallery of the Imperial Academy of Arts: Catalogue of the Paintings]. Saint Petersburg, 1874.

Speth-Holterhoff 1957
S. Speth-Holterhoff. *Les peintres flamands de cabinets d'amateurs.* Brussels, 1957.

Stechow 1966
W. Stechow. *Dutch Landscape Painting of the Seventeenth Century.* London, 1966.

Stechow 1969
————. "Some Observations on Rembrandt and Lastman." *Oud-Holland* 84, nos. 2–3 (1969), pp. 148–62.

Steland 1984
A. C. Steland. "Wasserfälle: Die Emanzipation eines Bildmotivs in der holländischen Malerei um 1640." *Niederdeutsche Beiträge zur Kunstgeschichte,* 1984, pp. 85–104.

Stroganoff 1793
Catalogue raisonné des tableaux qui composent la collection du comte A. de Stroganoff. Saint Petersburg, 1793.

Stroganoff 1800
Catalogues des tableaux qui composent la collection du comte A. de Stroganoff. Saint Petersburg, 1800.

Stuffman 1968
M. Stuffmann. "Les tableaux de la collection de Pierre Crozat." *Gazette des Beaux-Arts,* July–Sept. 1968.

Sumowski 1983
W. Sumowski. *Gemälde der Rembrandt-Schüler.* 3 vols. Landau (Pfalz), 1983.

Sutton 1984
P. Sutton et al. *Masters of Seventeenth Century Dutch Genre Painting* [exh. cat.: Philadelphia Museum of Art, March 18–May 13, 1984]. Philadelphia, 1984.

Tarasov 1983
Y. Tarasov. *Gollandskii peizazh XVII veka* [Seventeenth-century Dutch landscapes]. Moscow, 1983.

Tartakovskaya 1935
E. Tartakovskaya. *Ocherk gollandskoi zhivopisi XVII veka* [An essay on Dutch genre painting in the 18th century]. Leningrad, 1935.

Thiéry 1953
Y. Thiéry. *Le paysage flamand au XVIIe siècle*. Les peintres flamands du XVIIe siècle. Paris–Brussels–New York, 1953.

Trivas 1941
N. S. Trivas. *The Paintings of Frans Hals*. New York–London, 1941.

Trubnikov 1912
A. Trubnikov. "Kartiny Pavlovskogo dvortsa" [Paintings in the Pavlovsk Palace]. *Starye Gody*, Oct. 1912, pp. 17–28.

Tümpel 1968
C. Tümpel. "Ikonographische Beiträge zu Rembrandt." *Jahrbuch der Hamburger Kunstsammlungen* 13 (1968), pp. 95-126.

Tümpel 1974
A. Tümpel. "Claes Cornelisz Moeyaert." *Oud-Holland* 88, nos. 1–2 (1974), pp. 1–163 and no. 4, pp. 245–90.

Tümpel 1980
C. Tümpel. "Die Ikonographie der Amsterdamer Historienmalerei in der ersten Hälfte des 17. Jahrhunderts und die Reformation." *Vestigia Bibliae* 2 (1980), pp. 127–58.

Tümpel 1986
————. *Rembrandt: Mythos und Methode*. With additional texts by A. Tümpel. Königstein, 1986.

Ukazatel 1842
Ukazatel sobraniiu kartin. . . . [Guide to the painting collection. . . .]. Saint Petersburg, 1842.

Valentiner 1909
W. R. Valentiner. *Rembrandt: Des Meisters Gemälde*. Klassiker der Kunst. 3d ed. Stuttgart–Leipzig, 1909.

Valentiner 1921
————. *Rembrandt: Wiederaufgefundene Gemälde (1910–1920)*. Klassiker der Kunst, 27. Stuttgart–Berlin, 1921.

Valentiner 1923
————. *Frans Hals*. Klassiker der Kunst. 2d ed. Stuttgart–Berlin–Leipzig, 1923.

Valentiner 1930
————. "A Painter's Atelier by Michiel Sweerts." *Bulletin Detroit Institute of Art* 12 (1930).

Valentiner 1957
————. "Noch einmal *Die Judenbraut*." In *Festschrift Kurt Bauch*, pp. 229–30. Munich, 1957.

Varchavskaya 1963
M. Varchavskaya. *Van Deik: Kartiny v Ermitazhe* [Van Dyck: Paintings in the Hermitage]. Leningrad, 1963.

Varchavskaya 1967
————. "Certains traits particuliers de la décoration d'Anvers par Rubens pour l'entrée triomphale de l'Infant-Cardinal Ferdinand en 1635." *Bulletin des Musées Royaux des Beaux-Arts de Belgique*, 1967.

Varchavskaya 1975
————. *Kartiny Rubensa v Ermitazhe* [Rubens's paintings in the Hermitage]. Leningrad, 1975.

Varchavskaya 1981
————. "Rubens i antverpenskie romanisty: K voprosu ob istoricheskikh predposylkakh iskusstva Rubensa" [Rubens and the Antwerp novelists: On the historical prerequisites of Rubens's art]. In *Gosudarstvennyi Ermitazh, Zapadnoevropeiskoe iskusstvo XVII veka: Publikatsii i issledovaniia.* [State Hermitage, Western European art of the seventeenth century: Publications and studies]. Leningrad, 1981.

Vergara 1982
L. Vergara. *Rubens and the Poetics of Landscape*. New Haven, 1982.

Vertue 1930
[G. Vertue.] *Vertue Note Books* I. The Walpole Society, 18. Oxford, 1930.

Vertue 1938
[————.] *Vertue Note Books* II. The Walpole Society, 26. Oxford, 1938.

Vertue 1968
[————.] *Vertue Note Books* VI. The Walpole Society, 30. Oxford, 1968.

Vipper 1962
B. P. Vipper. *Otcherki gollandskoi zhivopisi epokhi rassveta* [Essays on Dutch painting of the Golden Age]. Moscow, 1962.

Volhard 1927
H. Volhard. *Die Grundtypen der Landschaftsbilder Jan van Goyens und ihre Entwicklung*. Doctoral dissertation, Halle, 1927.

Voorhelm-Schneevoogt 1873
C. G. Voorhelm-Schneevoogt. *Catalogue des estampes gravées d'après P. P. Rubens. . . .* Haarlem, 1873.

Voss 1905
H. Voss. "Rembrandt und Tizian." *Repertorium für Kunstwissenschaft* 28 (1905), pp. 156–62.

Vsevolozhskaya and Linnik 1975
S. Vsevolozhskaya and I. Linnik. *Caravaggio and His Followers*. Leningrad, 1975.

Waagen 1864
G. F. Waagen. *Die Gemäldesammlung in der Kaiserlichen Ermitage zu St. Petersburg nebst Bemerkungen über andere dortige Kunstsammlungen*. Munich, 1864. 2d ed., 1870.

Waal 1941
H. van de Waal. *Jan van Goyen*. Amsterdam, 1941.

Weisbach 1926
W. Weisbach. *Rembrandt*. Berlin, 1926.

Wilenski 1960
R. H. Wilenski. *Flemish Painters, 1430–1830*. 2 vols. London, 1960.

Willis [1911]
F. Willis. *Niederländische Marinemalerei*. Leipzig, [1911].

Winner 1961
M. Winner. "Zeichnungen des älteren Jan Brueghel." *Jahrbuch der Berliner Museen* 2, n.s. 3 (1961).

Wittrock 1974
I. Wittrock. "Abraham's Calling." *Konsthistorisk Tijdskrift* 43 (1974), pp. 8–19.

Wrangel 1913
N. Wrangel. "Iskusstvo i gosudar Nikolai Pavlovich" [Art and Czar Nikolai Pavlovich]. *Starye Gody*, July–Sept. 1913, pp. 53–63.

Wurzbach 1906–11
A. von Wurzbach. *Niederländisches Künstler-Lexikon*. 3 vols. Vienna–Leipzig, 1906–11. Reprint, Amsterdam, 1974.

Zolotov 1979
Y. K. Zolotov. *Georges de la Tour*. Moscow, 1979.